THE GOLF COURSE MILLIONAIRE

How To Turn Relationships into Big Business Through Golf

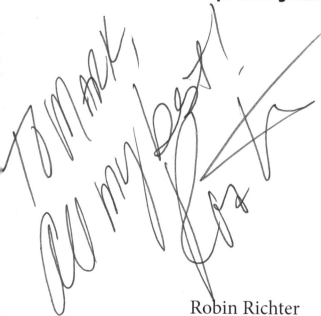

Robin Richter

ISBN 13: 9781980765875

TABLE OF CONTENTS

DEDICATION VII

FOREWORD BY ALLISON MASLAN IX

THE GOLF COURSE MILLIONAIRE
INTRODUCTION 1

ROBIN KRALL RICHTER
MY STORY 6

   The Early Days 6

   Going Pro. 7

   A Very Different Course 8

   A New Career 9

   #MeToo 10

   A New Beginning 11

   Too Good To Be True 11

   Truth to Power 13

   Justice 14

   A Cloud With A Silver Lining 15

   What's Next?. 16

   The Entrepreneurial Plunge 16

   Second Chances. 17

   Dad's Birthday Present to Me 19

   Record Growth. 20

   Success = Preparation + Opportunity 21

A Surrogate Father 22
The Hollywood Connection 25
Divine Providence 29
The Ultimate Relationship Builder 29

HYRUM W. SMITH **32**
Mentors And Lessons Learned 39
The Franklin Planner Success 41
Embracing Change – Grow With The Flow 42
Striking Out On Your Own –
The Entrepreneur 42
Sales Is Not A Dirty Word 44
The Value Of Integrity In Business 47

BETSY KING
LPGA HALL OF FAME GOLFER **53**

MICHAEL REES
CA OFFICE LIQUIDATORS **63**
A Lucrative Golf Connection 66
Character And Motivation 67
Connecting Through Golf 69
Put Me In, Coach! 70
Roadblocks & Analysis Paralysis 72

DONNA HOFFMAN
WOMEN ON COURSE **76**
A Non-Networking Networker 80
Where Do You Turn For Help? 82
Navigating Through Roadblocks 83
Women On Course For The Beginner 84
Women On Course – Different Strokes For Different
Folks 87

ROBERT FORT
INFORMATION TECHNOLOGY EXECUTIVE **91**

JENN HARRIS STREET SWING & HIGH HEEL GOLFER **106**

   Bringing Professional Women
   Into Golf. 107
   A Virtual Reality Golf Experience 108
   A Winning Attitude 111
   Value In Coaches & Mentors 113
   Grow With What You Know. 114
   Golf As A People Connector 115
   If I Knew Then What I Know Now. 116

PRACTICAL TIPS TO GET YOU STARTED FOR THE WOMEN:
FORWARD TEES ADVANTAGE 119

NETWORKING OPTIONS FOR NON-GOLFERS SPONSORSHIPS 121

   Sponsoring A Hole. 122
   Higher Level Sponsorships. 123
   No Cost Options! 124
   Networking Tips For Golfers
   Establish A Handicap 125
   Play As A Single & Hit The Driving Range 126
   Everyone Was Once A Beginner. 126

THERE ARE REALLY 19 HOLES IN GOLF!. 128

RESOURCE GUIDE 130

CONNECT WITH ROBIN 140

DEDICATION

In loving memory of my father, William Krall. When I was just nine years old, he inspired me to start playing the game of golf, which has contributed more to my life than I could ever include in a book.

My mother, Joan Krall, whose unconditional love continues to this day to be an example of how to live my life.

My husband, Matt Richter. Without his loving support and selfless devotion to our family, this book, and so many of the great things in my life would never have been possible.

My son, Joshua Richter, who is a daily reminder of God's true purpose for my life.

And my business coach and mentor, Allison Maslan, whose faith in my abilities and persistent encouragement finally convinced me to write this book.

FOREWORD BY ALLISON MASLAN

I received a call from a businesswoman who said she ran a promotional products company. She had seen a video about me on LinkedIn, talking about my business mentoring company. That woman was Robin Richter, and she was looking to hire a business coach. She wanted to meet me face-to-face to see if I was the right fit. Apparently, I was because that was over six years ago. It has been my honor to support Robin in her business growth and to enjoy her kind-heartedness as a dear friend.

We all know relationships in business are paramount. As the saying goes, it is not who you know; it is who knows you that moves your business forward. One good strategic relationship can multiply your growth overnight. That is where the *Golf Course Millionaire* comes in. I have written two business books and read countless others, so I can assure you this book won't disappoint.

Running a business is not easy. There are so many variables and aspects that a business owner must juggle. You have your revenue streams, marketing, sales, your team, and so much more. And that does not even include your personal life. You know that it is so important to get out and build relationships to take the big leaps, but you are often so buried in your work, and the thought of taking time away to play golf feels stressful and even overwhelming.

This is where Robin was several years ago. She was working away in her company and, although her business was doing well, the growth had become stagnant. What I realized in mentoring her was that she was spending all her time during the week behind her computer handling client engagements and orders. Yes, she was getting work done, but the way she was operating her company was creating incremental growth at best.

This is not an uncommon scenario. Business owners know the importance of relationships, yet they don't put the time in to foster their growth. When Robin told me that she had been a pro golfer in the past and that the golf course was one of her favorite places in the world, I knew that she was missing out on life and so much business opportunity! Not only is Robin a relationship ninja with the uncanny ability to talk to absolutely anyone and know their entire life story in a matter of minutes, but she is also an expert at golf, the perfect stomping ground for relationship building. From that time forward, Robin made the shift, and now spends several days a month building high-level relationships on the golf course. Spending the day getting to know successful CEOs has not only been a blast for Robin, but her closing ratio went way up. By doing so, her company is flourishing; she is building prosperous and interesting relationships on the course and adding more time back into her life.

What I do know after building ten companies over the last 30 years, is that doubling or tripling your revenues comes from relationships, not from working doubly hard. Growth comes from making the right strategic moves, and this generally involves meeting the right "who" person to open the doors for lucrative opportunities. It also goes beyond the finances to help you thrive as a happier human being.

The *Golf Course Millionaire* shares powerful strategies and inspiring stories from business owners who have used golf to propel their company forward. There is so much opportunity waiting for you right now. Enjoy *The Golf Course Millionaire: How to turn relationships into big business through the game of golf* so that you can be prepared for the high-net-worth CEOs you are about to meet.

Allison Maslan, CEO of Pinnacle Global Network Author of Scale or Fail, How to Leap from Entrepreneur to Enterprise.

Robin & Business Coach Allison Maslan

THE GOLF COURSE MILLIONAIRE
Introduction

This book has been evolving in my head for many years, waiting for the right time to come out. My passion for the game of golf runs deep because of the many ways it has enhanced my life. Without golf, I would not have developed the many amazing friendships that began on the course. Without golf, I would not have grown my successful promotional products business of 26 years. And most importantly, without golf I would have never met my incredible husband, Matt, the father of my amazing son, Joshua, and my trusted partner in business. My life without golf is very difficult to imagine. This is not to say that golf IS my life. Instead, golf has helped me to make a life for myself that is extremely fulfilling in so many ways. The people I've met, the opportunities I've had, and the lessons I've learned through golf have made me a stronger, happier, and more successful person.

Robin, Matt and Josh with his best friend, Cole

Chances are you are reading this book because on some level, you are interested in golf and possibly growing your business. The information contained in my book will help you discover very effective ways to enhance and improve your life and your career through golf. You will find valuable nuggets of golf and professional career inspiration that will put you on the road to greater financial success. If you are a non-golfer, my goal is to help you remove the self-imposed barriers of intimidation that have kept you off the course. I have also provided effective networking strategies I've used on the golf course that you can use without ever picking up a club. And when you finally do learn to play, you will be able to apply many more lessons learned in this book and transform your relationships on the course into opportunities for success!

In the following pages, you will hear from six uniquely successful people who have used golf to one degree or another to define themselves in their lives or their careers. Hyrum Smith is the entrepreneur behind the billion-dollar company *Franklin Quest*. He took up golf at almost 50 years old when his business began sponsoring *PGA Tournaments* in the early 90s. Through these tournament sponsorships, he had the good fortune of developing close personal relationships with some of the major pro golfers of his time, including Gary Player, Jack Nicklaus, and Tom Watson. He shared with me some of his valuable wisdom gained both on the course and in the boardroom.

Betsy King is an *LPGA Hall of Famer* and one of the top ten women golfers in the world. In addition to playing on the *LPGA Senior Tour,* she is passionate about promoting her charity, *Golf Fore Africa.* Betsy uses her golf fame to connect with potential donors and benefactors to raise funds for poor undeveloped countries in Africa. In 2006, after a life-changing trip, Betsy founded the non-profit organization, *Golf Fore Africa.* Its mission is to bring hope and change to children and families living in extreme poverty in Africa by empowering the golf community to support transformational programs that holistically enhance the families they serve. Betsy uses her experience and connections in golf to enlist golfers around the world to join the cause.

Mike Rees is a seasoned entrepreneur and the President of *CA Office Liquidators* in San Diego. An avid golfer who learned to play with his family as a young kid, Mike has a genuine love for the game. In his career, he has used golf to make connections and create lasting business alliances. He has taken the mystery out of networking on the golf course by initiating his own golf events and targeting players with common professional interests. Mike explained how golf is a very effective way to get to know the authentic person. "There have been times when I've wished I had the opportunity to play golf with people before doing business with them. It may have motivated me to form a beneficial business alliance earlier, or warned me to avoid getting into a less than ideal arrangement. Show me a person's golf game, and I'll show you who that person really is."

Donna Hoffman is the founder of *Events19* and *Women on Course*. Established in 2005, *Women on Course* is the fastest growing women's golf community, helping women golfers feel comfortable and confident participating in the golf lifestyle. As a former television producer, Donna learned to play golf in her mid-40s. She loved golf so much, she carved out her post-television production career from her growing affinity for the game. From new and learning golfers to seasoned players, she has engaged thousands in the sport, providing everything from basic beginner instruction to organizing social and business golf trips.

Robert Fort is an internationally recognized and awarded IT innovator with over 30 years of Information Technology experience. He has served as SVP and CIO for several large corporations in Southern California. His inspiring and effective leadership style makes him a highly sought after motivational mentor and speaker to many businesses and professionals. In the 1990s, Robert became increasingly aware of the social value of golf in business, and was introduced to the game by business associates. He quickly became captivated with the sport, the camaraderie and the lifestyle, and has played regularly ever since. His experience on the golf course has helped him to grow both personally and professionally, while providing a great networking venue along the way.

Jen Harris is a young entrepreneur and golf enthusiast who left the corporate world to pursue her dream of sharing her love of golf with others. As an avid golfer, she has spent the past six years bringing the game to non-golfers and showing them how golf can improve their lives by helping them build lasting and rewarding relationships. In 2012, Jenn founded *High Heel Golfer*, an organization that strives to connect and inspire women to achieve their personal and professional goals through the game of golf. More recently, Jenn founded *Street Swing*, a traveling virtual reality golf experience that brings golf directly to clients and their event venues.

Finally, there is my story. I open this book with my story so that you can see how golf has truly shaped the person I am today. After reading this first chapter, I believe it will make perfect sense why I wrote this book. I am so grateful for all the wonderful blessings that golf has brought to my life. I hope that you, too, will benefit from the tremendous opportunities that golf can provide in your life.

ROBIN KRALL RICHTER
My Story

THE EARLY DAYS

I was born in Chester, Pennsylvania where I grew up the middle child of three girls. My father was an engineer for a major chemical company, and my mother was a devoted homemaker. To some extent, because of golf, I played the role of the son my father never had. When I was a young girl, we belonged to a country club where my dad played golf while his girls went swimming and lounged by the pool. When he drove by after playing the seventh hole, I would run out and jump in the cart, hoping he would let me drive, which he often did. As a kid, I always thought this was the best time ever! Before long, Dad handed me a golf club and showed me how to hit the ball. From the beginning, it was evident that God blessed me with some natural talent. Since my dad had such a love for golf, he was enthused to discover my abilities and, before long, he enrolled me in golf lessons. We left Pennsylvania for Southern California when I was nine years old. The mild climate meant more time for golf. Little did I know at that time that a decade later, I would be attending college on a full-ride golf scholarship, and soon after graduation, I would be competing professionally on the Women's Professional Golf Tour (WPGT). At that point in my young life, the opportunity to pursue a career in professional golf was there for the taking.

I think that my dad wanted my career as a golf pro more for me than I wanted it for myself. He saw this talent in me, and by encouraging me to pursue golf, he was vicariously living his dream. He loved golf more than anything. He lived and breathed it. He spent a lot of time out in the garage cleaning his clubs and organizing his bag. His life pretty much revolved around his Wednesday golf game with the guys. My dad was an average golfer; he fluctuated between a 15 and an 18 handicap, which is very respectable. From time to time, I would play in his men's group on Wednesdays, and I hold some very special memories in my heart from those days. I think he was always proud to show me off to his friends whenever we played together.

GOING PRO

After I graduated college, my dad encouraged me to turn pro. He became my sponsor, which proved that he had a great deal of faith in my abilities. Being my sponsor gave us a new common interest. My competing in golf became his new hobby. At first, playing pro and going on tour was exciting. But after a while, it lost its novelty, and I began to enjoy it less. I am a people person and, in college, where golf was a team sport, I thrived on the energy and spirit. But on the tour, each player stood alone competing individually. So the camaraderie just didn't exist on the tour like it did in my college days. I was on the road traveling a lot, staying in hotels, and at other peoples' houses by myself. Eventually, the isolation of traveling and competing solo caused me to become very lonely.

During the break from my touring schedule, I decided to get a part-time job to make some money and keep myself busy when I wasn't competing. During the break, I went to the Broadway Department Store to apply for a job. They offered me a sales position in their cosmetics department, which I happily accepted. I found the work to be super enjoyable, and I quickly developed close personal relationships with the other ladies in the cosmetics department. This job had the teamwork piece that I was missing on the tour. I am definitely a people person and would much rather be part of a team than go it alone. As a social type, the personal one-on-one consultations that I provided my clients proved to be very rewarding. Helping my clients feel better about themselves brought me such joy. I discovered that lifting people up in such a personal way and making them feel good about themselves was extremely fulfilling. I found that I really loved the process of building up the sale from a bottle of perfume to include skincare, makeup, and more. I have always loved dealing with people and, in particular, helping people. So all this interaction had energized me and caused me to thrive!

A VERY DIFFERENT COURSE

Through my experiences working in what I thought to be a temporary cosmetics sales position, it became apparent very quickly that I needed to pursue a different path. While I really enjoyed golf, turning the hobby into a career took a lot of the fun out of it. I was social by nature and being a golf pro just didn't seem to fit my personality at that stage of my life. I was still fairly young, and I needed to be part of a team. My newfound friends could see that I was torn between returning to the tour and pursuing a different career and they encouraged me to follow my dreams. Deep down, I always knew that I belonged in sales. Time was running out, and I had to make a decision. There were only a few weeks left before I was expected back on tour. I'll never forget the day I told my parents I was hanging up my clubs for a while. Up to that point, it was probably the worst day of my life. I sat down with my parents in our living room to announce a hiatus in my pro-golf career. I explained to them how much I loved my new job and how lonely I was on the professional golf tour. My dad was devastated. He really took it personally. He was emotionally invested in my pro-golf career, and I had let him down. He barely spoke to me for the next three months. He told his friends, "Oh, she doesn't play golf anymore; she sells lipsticks." It was a very difficult time in our relationship. But eventually, we both came to realize that God had another plan for me. And years later, we would become business partners once again.

A NEW CAREER

What started out as a job selling fragrances turned into a lucrative, ten-year sales career in the cosmetics industry with a well-known cosmetics company. And although my dad was disappointed that I left what could have been a very successful pro-golf career, he grew to become very proud of my accomplishments in the business world. After my entrée into the cosmetics industry, Broadway began carrying a brand new line of cosmetics called Lancôme. They hired me as their first counter manager, and I worked my way up the corporate ladder before being hired as Lancôme's first ever Account Coordinator. I became a very skilled salesperson, able to turn a lipstick transaction into the sale of an entire skincare line. From there, I was promoted to Account Executive, selling to the small drug store chains. Eventually, I came full circle and ended up working as the Lancôme Account Executive for all 21 of the Southern California Broadway Department Stores. Through several promotions, I was awarded a great deal of responsibility with over 100 beauty advisors in my charge. My time was spent traveling to all the department stores, negotiating the open-to-buy with the head cosmetic buyers, while also providing sales training to the beauty advisors. I loved motivating the sales associates and showing them how to develop relationships and build a sale. For the first time, I was truly in my element.

#METOO

One day in the late eighties, I was at the driving range hitting balls. A man came up to me and asked, "Hey, is your name Robin Krall?" I said, "Yes." He told me that he remembered seeing me play on tour. He asked me what I was doing these days, and that led to a conversation about my job and his business. He owned a company that sold golf equipment, and he was looking to hire a Marketing Director to negotiate the contracts with the golf-pros and to help grow the branded golf ball division. His company sponsored pros on tour and paid these professionals a royalty for wearing apparel or using equipment on which his corporate logo was imprinted. Royalty deals would fluctuate based on certain factors such as logo placement and the level of the pro. Knowing my background in pro-golf and also in sales, he offered me the position right there on the spot, asserting, "You are exactly the person I am looking for to fill this spot." I politely declined, explaining that I was very satisfied with my current career path and wasn't looking to make a change.

Over the next several weeks, he persisted in his attempts to recruit me as his Marketing Director. I was tempted because I missed golf and I loved the affinity concept of the logo marketing sponsorships. Plus, I missed working with men. Finally, he asked, "What's it going to take to get you to come work for me? Give me a number." So to discourage him, I threw out a very large salary with benefits and conditions, thinking he would dismiss the idea. Surprisingly, he agreed to my salary requirements and, having agreed to meet all my conditions, including working from home, which was my workplace set-up at the time, I accepted his offer.

A NEW BEGINNING

I had an absolute blast in the beginning. I was given the project of developing the logoed golf ball line with some really unique packaging. The boss said, "How can we build this line and how can we sell it to more corporations?" So, I developed a strategy to build a product line from their popular golf balls and a marketing plan to get maximum exposure for increased sales.

One of the things I learned about was this industry called ASI, (Advertising Specialty Industry). In the ASI industry, a product supplier takes its product line to distributors, who then present it to corporate clients and get orders to produce customized versions of products, personalized with corporate logos. So, to exploit this new market, I had a booth made, created a compelling golf ball display, and took a couple of people out to the trade show in Chicago. The show generated a ton of leads. I began working these by sending out product samples in direct marketing campaigns. We landed some very large corporate clients. The experience started off great. I met a bunch of industry people and established some good business relationships. We increased sales in that department five-fold from $60,000 to over $300,000 in nine months. I was really enjoying my new job. I loved the whole concept of branding. I also enjoyed negotiating sponsorships with the pros. This experience had turned me on to an industry where I could indulge my love of golf in a way that utilized my talent in sales and my knack for relationship building. I was definitely on to something!

TOO GOOD TO BE TRUE

In retrospect, the warning signs were revealed early on, but I was still young and I didn't recognize them right away. We initially had an agreement that I would work from my home office. As a sales professional, I was accustomed to working from home when

I wasn't on the road for appointments, sales training, and trade shows. As a condition of employment, he agreed that I would enjoy that same flexibility. However, once I started, he failed to keep his word. From the beginning, he urged me to work at the office, always promising it would be temporary until I was fully trained. My presence at the office was essentially unnecessary. But he insisted I be there and, over time, it became easier to comply than to resist. So the work from home arrangement never actually panned out. After six months, I began to realize he was an unusually controlling boss.

There were some additional problems in the early days and somehow my attractive salary was not kept confidential from the other employees. Some of the team questioned my employment contract and why I was one of the highest paid employees in the company. Suspicion led to speculation about the nature of my relationship with the boss. There were gossip and innuendo, and this made the working environment increasingly uncomfortable.

To compound the situation, gradually, the boss began inviting me to functions away from the office, claiming them to be work-related. I started to realize the inappropriateness of his increasing social demands when he invited me to his home, adding, "Oh, and bring your bathing suit! We'll go for a Jacuzzi." It became a minefield where I was constantly trying to avoid being put in compromising situations, without offending my boss. But he was a very controlling person. Up until that point, I had a high degree of confidence handling myself in a variety of stressful situations, both on the golf course and off. But as a young woman, I had never before experienced anything like this, and I didn't know how to deal with it.

The situation finally came to a head when we all attended the PGA show in Orlando Florida. Under his exhausting manipulation, I found myself in a terrible situation where he tried to take advantage of me physically. I would rather not go into detail at this point, but I will say it was the worst night of my life. I ended up having to flee his presence to avoid being assaulted or worse. In the midst of the chaos, I left my purse behind. Making my way back to my room, I was frightened and disgusted. Thankfully, the colleague with whom I was rooming was there because in leaving my purse behind, I had no key. I went straight to the bathroom and started vomiting. I was under so much stress, it was making me physically sick. I had never felt that kind of pressure before. I had no idea what I was going to do.

The boss had arranged for a group of fifteen of us to meet the next morning for breakfast. I told my colleague, "I can't go. I'm afraid of him." She urged, "You have to go, or the situation will get worse. Besides, you need to get your purse. Just act like nothing happened." So, I remember just sitting there in the restaurant, terrified. There I was with all the others, waiting for this arrogant and manipulative narcissist to arrive. He made his grand entrance into the restaurant dangling my purse in his hand, for all to see. He yelled out, "Hey, Krall, you forgot this last night." I was terrified and humiliated. It was a very demeaning situation I found myself in, and I had done nothing to encourage his horrible abuse.

TRUTH TO POWER

When I finally got home from that business trip, I had to regroup and leave immediately for a scheduled event in Palm Springs. I was still emotionally distressed over what happened in Florida, but I mistakenly thought I could drive the experience and the anxiety away through the distraction of busyness. While in Palm Springs, I tried my best to hold it together. But I got to a point where I just couldn't go on and act as if nothing had happened. I literally broke down crying. I was such a mess; I couldn't even drive my car. I had to call my mom and ask her to come and get me. This was not par for the course for my personality. I was a strong and successful young woman with a high degree of self-confidence before I began working for this man. But as many victims of serial sexual harassers learn, the predator is skilled at undermining the very self-confidence that would ordinarily protect a woman from becoming a victim in the first place. Over the two years at his company, he succeeded in slowly chipping away at my self-confidence until I began to question my own instincts. Then in Florida, he went for the kill and defeated every ounce of confidence I had left. He wasn't about to let me beat him at his game.

Seeing how upset I was, my mom got me home and took me to a highly respected and recommended psychologist. This woman helped me to come to terms with what happened and formulate a plan to leave my job in such a way that I would be his last victim.

JUSTICE

Over the next three weeks, I meticulously carried out the plan, gathering enough evidence to prove his sexual harassment in court if necessary. Then I made my break with his company and filed suit. It was very frightening. He grew bolder and bolder and began pulling stunts to threaten my safety in both words and strong-arm tactics. There were times I was fearful for my life. I had been followed; my property had been destroyed; my car was vandalized, and the list goes on. In those days, there weren't phones and surveillance cameras everywhere. So his intimidation went mostly unchecked. He was trying to get me to drop the suit by intimidating me. The only way I was able to stay on course was to focus on the bigger picture. I didn't want anyone else ever to suffer the way I had. I wanted to put an end to his abuse. The high drama and threatening activities continued for over a year while the lawsuit was pending. The depositions that I was required to give were designed to intimidate, frustrate, and completely twist the facts to make him look innocent. But I had firm resolve to see this through. Somehow, word got out about the lawsuit, and I was contacted by a number of prior victims who described their similar ordeals. Their corroborating stories reinforced the fact that I was doing the right thing.

Just before the trial, I was strongly encouraged by a court-appointed mediator to settle. In a reality check, I was reminded that a jury would determine the fate of this trial. At that time, because of sexual harassment stories in the national media, juries were suspicious of these lawsuits and not very sympathetic to victims of sexual harassment. Despite the facts of the case, the verdict could go either way. I was also warned that his attorneys would attempt to drag my entire family through the mud and nothing would be off limits. I had no doubt that was true, based on the stunts he had pulled up to that point. The opposing team might fabricate stories to try and challenge my claims and impugn my credibility. Or even worse, they might try to hurt my family. I was warned that if I pursued the trial and lost, I would come out the other end worse off. After all I had been through, I couldn't bear the thought of losing. I reluctantly agreed to settle.

A CLOUD WITH A SILVER LINING

The most gratifying thing for me happened at the end of this ordeal when we were walking out of the courthouse, and the lead attorney of his four-man legal team came up to me and said, "You know what? You did the right thing. I just hope that this is the last straw for this guy because I'm done." Hearing that attorney speak those words about his own client validated every injustice that I felt that year. It made the whole ordeal worth it. In the end, I knew I had done the right thing and, as a result, I could only hope that this man would think twice before he ever harmed or abused another woman again. #MoreThanASurvivor

WHAT'S NEXT?

After leaving the golf equipment company, I took a position as an Account Executive selling premium-incentive lead-generation direct mail packages to the automobile industry. I pitched a proposal to dealerships that involved my company sending out lead-generating direct mail packages, offering high end, premium gifts as an incentive to get them into the dealership to test drive a car. These very effective packages were a high-priced ticket at $14,000, but the break-even rate was more than achievable because these packages generated a ton of dealership traffic. With a decent closing rate, the dealer could recoup its advertising expense and turn a substantial profit fairly easily. This was a suitable interim position while I was engaged with attorneys and depositions as we prepped for litigation. But after I settled my legal affairs, I realized that this was not going to satisfy my long-term career desires.

THE ENTREPRENEURIAL PLUNGE

I was at a crossroads with some important decisions to make. First, I took inventory of my professional experience, assets, and preferences. I wanted my next move to have roots and sustain me for the long haul. I had ten years' experience in high-level sales and contract negotiations with a major international cosmetic company. Going on tour as a golf pro gave me practical golf experience on the course and valuable contacts off. My two years spent as Marketing Director at the golf equipment company provided me the opportunity to pursue corporate golf sponsorships and introduced me to the advertising specialty industry. And the Account Executive position at the direct marketing company taught me about using premium gifts as sales incentives in direct marketing campaigns. As a golf pro, I had worked as an independent agent. As an account executive in the cosmetic industry, I had corporate experience. And as Marketing Director for a golf equipment company, I had a taste of the entrepreneurial experience. Being a driven creative type, I definitely had the entrepreneurial appetite and wanted to start my own promotional products company. But I didn't even know where to begin.

By that time, my dad had gained a lot of professional respect for me over the dozen years since I left the golf tour. He saw me work my way up through corporate America and make something of myself while gaining valuable experience. He was thrilled when I re-entered the golf industry through the back door of a supplier. And when I left that position amidst a lengthy legal challenge, he was very supportive and understood why I had to leave. So I came up with a plan. I took an apprentice type position working for a man who owned his own promotional product business. After about a year, I felt very confident in the additional experience I had gained, and I was ready to launch my own business. I needed capital and, at the time, my dad was somewhat newly retired and looking for a place to spend his time and some investment money. I presented him with a business plan for a partnership in 1992. He agreed, and Wearable Imaging, Inc. was founded, which is in its 26th year of business today.

SECOND CHANCES

After all the strife my father and I had been through when I left my career as a golf pro, this was finally another opportunity for a joint venture with my dad. Eager and excited, we developed this business together, and it really took off. I had the youthful energy, sales know-how, and contacts. Dad, as a retired engineer, had the discipline, the investment capital, the willingness, and the time. We had so many great times together building up the business and celebrating its impressive growth. These cherished memories are so very special to me, and I am grateful for all the wonderful blessings.

Sadly, I lost my dad back in 2005, shortly after he was diagnosed with a rare disease that took him prematurely and unexpectedly. It was a devastating time in my life. My dad and I had such a unique bond that was uncommon to most father/daughter relationships that I knew. Thankfully, my husband Matt agreed to leave his career and join Wearable Imaging, Inc. full time to fill the deep hole left by my father's passing. Today, Matt has been my business partner for over a dozen years. I am blessed that I have been able to keep this venture in the family.

Robin and her dad

DAD'S BIRTHDAY PRESENT TO ME

A few months after losing my dad, I happened to be playing in a charity golf tournament. We teed off on a par three, which happened to be the first hole for our group. It was a blind shot, meaning the hole was not visible from the tee. I was the first one to hit. I remember hitting the shot and thinking, "Wow! That was solid! I'm sure I'm on the green." We walked up after everyone hit their shots and I couldn't find my ball. I walked past the green and started looking in the bushes, but my ball was nowhere to be found. I said to my friend, Jane, "I could've sworn I hit a great shot, but my ball's not here!" She said, "Maybe it's in the hole!" I thought she was joking and replied, "Yeah, very funny." So she said, "No, I mean it! Where could it be? It's not around here. Let's go look in the hole." So as we approached the hole, I just remember my heart pounding. We looked in the hole, and sure enough, my ball was there. I had hit a hole in one! My first hole in one in all the years I'd been playing. I was still a little raw after the shock and mourning since the death of my dad. So realizing that I had hit my first hole in one was a stunning revelation!! When the ladies in my group caught on, they began to scream and cheer wildly. Jane, who is an amazing golf pro and happens to be my instructor to this day, said, "Your dad kicked it in the hole for you because he knew you were coming up on your 50th birthday. That was his birthday gift to you." That was an amazing moment. Whenever I think of my dad, I remember that hole in one and smile.

Hole-in One at Strawberry Farms

RECORD GROWTH

Through the launch and early phases of the business, I continued to get out there and play golf in charity tournaments with clients, even though I was incredibly busy growing the business. I was still a decent player, maintaining a single digit handicap, and still able to play and build relationships with some major corporate execs. I had made many high-level connections in major corporations such as Toyota, Pepsi, BMW, and Lexus, to name a few. I would never have been able to get into these companies if not for the golf connections. The people who play in charity tournaments are usually high-level executives; I was constantly being paired with these corporate decision makers and influencers because I would go in as a single or they would put me in as the celebrity pro. There were just so many great opportunities to get to know these people on a deeper level and create lasting bonds.

Most of the time, these corporate contacts were much higher on the organizational chart than those responsible for the purchasing of promotional products. The CEO or CFO would share with me some high-level corporate information and then direct me to the appropriate middle management employee, saying, "You need to call this guy and be sure to tell him I sent you." I loved making the initial contact at the highest levels. Then when I called the marketing director, and said, "Hi, your boss told me to call you," he had no choice but to take the call and at least give me the time to show him how I could help meet his objectives.

SUCCESS = PREPARATION + OPPORTUNITY

Given the opportunity to present proposals and plans, Wearable Imaging's sales conversion rate is very high, relative to industry standards. I attribute this to my company's ability to match our clients with the most popular, cutting-edge promotional products to meet their corporate objectives. Whether it's a low-cost mass marketing alternative to business cards, an elaborate, high-end, designer "swag bag," or something in between, we always find that relevant promotional gifts designed to wow the intended audience can transform a corporate brand into a cultural buzzword. I've traveled to the other side of the globe to source the most unique and compelling gifts so that we know just the right thing to offer when a client needs something super special. It is my top priority to have a solid read on the pulse of the latest and greatest in cool gift ideas and to stay abreast of the most fashionable culture trends – before they even happen.

Over the past 26 years since founding Wearable Imaging, Inc., the steady growth of our business has provided us with the purchasing power to leverage competitive pricing for the benefit of our client base. We are confident in our ability to match our clients with the most successful promotional products at highly competitive prices, especially considering the superior quality of the products we provide.

In addition, I have acted as an integral part of many corporate marketing teams in executing plans that aim to grow a base, generate leads, expand brand awareness, increase sales, and re-brand a decades-old established household name. My experience in meeting a diverse number of corporate objectives while overcoming a wide variety of challenges is a huge asset and makes our company effective consultants and strategists to our clients.

The bottom line is that Wearable Imaging is prepared to meet any challenge and exceed expectations when called upon to perform for our clients. When an opportunity presents itself, we are ready! Our track record of being prepared for opportunities precipitates even more opportunities! This is a major factor in our continued success. This is a critical life lesson that I would like to pass along, not only to younger generations of family and friends but also to you. If you want to be successful, invest in your preparation. Make yourself ready for that chance of a lifetime! Everyone gets a lucky break now and again. The difference between success and failure is in the preparation. Be prepared and, when that opportunity comes, you will hit a hole in one!

A SURROGATE FATHER

Early on in my business career, when I was still figuring out what to do with my life, I met the most amazing man. His name was Bud Gordon, and at the time I met him, he owned a Toyota dealership. I was invited by Toyota to be one of the celebrities in a golf tournament, and Bud was in my foursome. We had a great time getting to know each other over five hours spent on the course. At that time, I had just taken the Account Executive position selling lead-generation, direct-mail packages to the automobile industry. I was brand new in this sales position when I reached out to Bud, whom I had remembered from the golf tournament months earlier. He asked me to call him back in three months after I was fully trained.

Exactly three months to the day, I called him and said, "Hi, Bud! Remember me? You told me to call you back in three months." We agreed to meet for lunch. He made reservations at a fancy Italian restaurant. I showed up with my presentation materials which, in the days before laptops, consisted of a flipchart sales proposal. I began to deliver my canned presentation when Bud interrupted me, "Put your flipchart away. You've already got the deal. What is this going to cost me?" I replied, "$14,000, but I haven't even given you any details." He replied, "You had the deal three months ago. It's done. I trust you." This perfectly illustrates the amazing power of golf. Bud got to know me in a way that is unique to the golf experience. Those five hours on the golf course months earlier were enough for him to trust his instincts about me.

Bud Gordon

Bud turned out to be one of my closest friends, confidants, and mentors. He and I formed an amazing friendship, and he was like a second father to me. He taught me so much about corporate America: how to conduct myself with the general managers of the dealerships; what to say; and what not to say. He taught me some great marketing strategies. We played in dozens of corporate tournaments together, to which he would always invite me. Together, we won over 15 tournaments over the course of our 20 plus year friendship. The tournament prizes were numerous. We won televisions, stereos, golf clubs, airfare; you name it!

Bud was an extremely generous man. It seemed that every time we were at these charity events, he would drop thousands of dollars bidding on live and silent auction items. He would often give away his prizes as incentives to his employees or reuse them to generate additional revenue for the charities that he sponsored. He had such a passion for giving back and often in the most unique ways. In fact, he was the creative genius behind the mini-museum Quality West Wing in Corona, California. It was an interactive presidential museum experience that housed a one of a kind replica of the Oval Office. Over 200,000 students visited this place where they learned many interesting facts about the executive branch of our government. His inspiration for hiring a Hollywood set designer to create this Oval Office replica was his desire to educate youth about government and politics. He recognized that there was a need, and instead of complaining about what's missing, he rolled up his sleeves and got it done. He was one of the most amazing people I have ever had the pleasure to know. Bud Gordon was truly one of a kind.

Those were just some really fun years. Bud went on to buy several dealerships over the years and continued to introduce me to his dealer friends. I adored his family and eventually when I got married and had a son, he was just like a grandfather to Joshua. After I lost my dad, he became a proxy father figure. Bud was always there for me. Sadly, he developed a serious illness a few years back and passed away. It was just devastating losing him, especially after losing my father. I know he and my dad are both still with me in spirit. I'm sure they're playing golf in heaven – especially when I'm out on the golf course. I can feel their presence. It may seem very strange, but I do!

B. Krall   J. McAlpin   N. Alden   R. Krall   B. Gordon

Robin with her mentors

THE HOLLYWOOD CONNECTION

Back in the late 90s, I played in a Boy Scouts of America charity golf tournament. Their big fundraiser was a silent auction, where attendees could bid on various prizes that were donated to the non-profit. One such prize was a walk-on part on the CBS primetime medical drama, *Chicago Hope*. I won! When the time came to redeem the prize, my husband and I showed up at the studio where we first had to clear security. The ID Office, located in a studio back lot trailer, was a place to get photographed and have a temporary ID made. While we were there, I noticed about twenty framed photographs hanging on the walls. Each picture featured the same woman, always dressed in a stylish golf outfit with various celebrities. Being a golfer, I was immediately curious, so I asked the studio staff person, "Who is this woman?" I learned that her name was Linda and she was the medical advisor on the show. It was her job to help make the medical parts of the script realistic by bringing her expertise to the set. Based on these photographs, this woman seemed to have a golf connection to dozens of Hollywood celebrities!

Later that day, we were having lunch in the studio commissary. I noticed a familiar face and, realizing it was the medical advisor Linda from the golf photos, I went over and introduced myself. I explained that I recognized her from the photographs in the ID Office. I told her how impressed I was that she knew everyone and, more importantly, she had played golf with all of these famous people. We started talking about golf and immediately started to develop a friendship. Before we parted ways, she asked me for my phone number, promising to reach out so we could play golf sometime. Little did I know that I would eventually work closely with Linda. I have come to greatly admire her for she is such a genuine, warm, and giving person. She always has a smile on her face. Today, I consider her to be one of the warmest, most wonderful people I know. I truly adore her.

As promised, several weeks after meeting Linda, she called me to invite me to the *Chicago Hope Golf Tournament*. Little did I know at the time that this would turn into a major opportunity for me to break into the entertainment industry. At the golf tournament, Linda so graciously connected me to *David E. Kelly Productions*, where we ended up producing promotional products for *Ally McBeal* and *The Practice*. Wearable Imaging eventually provided all the promotional products for the shows and their golf tournaments. When *Chicago Hope* went off the air in 2000, Linda called me and said, "Hey, we're doing this pilot for a TV show called *Grey's Anatomy*. I'm not sure if it's going to get picked up, but we need promotional products for the pilots – lanyards and mugs with the hospital name on them. I need these in three days. Can you make this happen?" So, of course, I replied, "Yes. No problem!" We got the order turned around fast and everything shipped to arrive before the deadline.

A few months later, I received a call from Linda. She was very excited as she announced that *Grey's Anatomy* was picked up by ABC to be a part of their prime time line up. Since 2005, we have been providing all of their swag, including personalized items used on the set; all of their VIP giveaways; and cast and crew Christmas gifts. I visit the studio several times during the season to meet with them to identify and fulfill their needs. It's been a huge blessing and just so much fun. All of that happened because of the connections that I made through golf. Linda is just the warmest, most wonderful person. There's no way I would have ever met Linda through ordinary circumstances. Golf has been the most amazing connector for me.

Linda Klein with cast and crew of CBS hit show, Grey's Anatomy

Robin and Katie with Grey's Anatomy *Cast*

DIVINE PROVIDENCE

I have always believed that God has a plan and His plan for me has somehow consistently involved golf. Golf seems to be the mechanism for so many good things in my life. And in my younger days, when I wasn't sure how much I wanted to immerse myself in this sport, God helped me to find the proper balance so that I could ultimately use golf as a way to serve Him. Golf has enhanced my life in so many ways and has given me this incredible opportunity to start my own business and watch it thrive. I feel so blessed and have made it a practice to share the fruits of my labor with others, especially those less fortunate and those who suffer. There is no way I would have grown the business so successfully if not for my faith in God and the connections made through this wonderful thing called golf. Connecting golf to the Creator of the universe might seem a little gratuitous for some, but it's not for me. The natural beauty of the outdoors is a constant reminder of God's perfection in the world. Every time I play, whether it is on an ocean course or out in the desert terrain, I am reminded of His presence and filled with gratitude. God is GOOD!

THE ULTIMATE RELATIONSHIP BUILDER

Success is great, but in life, it's relationships that truly matter. While material success makes a person secure and can provide many comforts, especially in times of trial, it's really those people with whom you build lasting relationships that bring true meaning to life. As committed as I am to my business, it's these relationships that make my work so fulfilling. And golf has been the major conduit to build those incredible bonds. When I think of my clients in those terms, serving them becomes a labor of love. And as the saying goes, "Love what you do, and you'll never work a day in your life."

By now, you have probably recognized the recurring theme that golf is a great way to get to know people on a more meaningful level. Everyone I have interviewed for this book has pointed out that golf provides something much greater than mere "networking." Not enough can be said about the incredible value of relationship building that golf provides. When you spend five hours on the golf course with someone, you begin to see them in ways that you cannot know through business meetings or the occasional lunch. On the course, you witness how a person reacts and responds to victory, defeat, challenges, and disappointments. It is enlightening as to the character of a person who graciously accepts victory and praise, even consoling and encouraging his opponent. When playing as a team as in the case of a scramble, you get to strategize together, and it can be an amazing team-building exercise. You also have so much time for conversation that, by the end of the day, you can know a lot about a person's family, career, childhood, dreams, and more! And because the atmosphere on the course is so relaxing and peaceful, it's really such a great backdrop to unwind and share some recreational fun.

It has been almost 50 years since I first picked up a golf club back in Chester, Pennsylvania. Over the past half-century, I have played on so many golf courses all over the world. And through those years, I have competed in over a hundred charity tournaments and built dozens of strong relationships on the golf course. Because of my skill level and strong connections to golf, I am frequently invited to charity tournaments. Each new tournament is another opportunity to create relationships. I recently was given the privilege to accompany the competitors inside the rope at the Toshiba Classic Pro Golf Tournament. It was quite a thrill watching the pros up close and hanging with them at the end. Two different clients have invited me to play in big charity tournaments in the coming weeks. There is no doubt that these will be great opportunities to make new connections and sow the seeds to forge relationships that will bear valuable fruit down the line. I anticipate every opportunity with much gratitude and will always look for ways to serve and give back. Because of golf, my life has been abundantly blessed. I hope yours will be abundantly blessed too!

HYRUM W. SMITH

https://www.hyrumwsmith.com

Robin with Hyrum W. Smith

Hyrum **W. Smith** *in corporate circles is described as the "Father of Time Management" and is probably associated in the minds of most people with what was Franklin Quest and is now Franklin Covey. As the co-founder of these companies, he was directly responsible for training over six million people throughout the course of his career in time management and personal productivity. He was the time management guru, or more accurately put, the life management specialist. He "retired" from Franklin in 2004 to pursue other interests. He has since written many books including* You Are What You Believe, The 3 Gaps, *and* What Matters Most.

I recently had the opportunity to chat with Hyrum, and he shared with me many of his philosophies about business, networking, and of course, golf. Hyrum is not only a highly successful businessman, he is an excellent golfer – but he didn't start out that way. In 1997, his company, Franklin Quest acquired the Covey Leadership Center (founded by Stephen R. Covey) and is now known as Franklin Covey. In the years preceding the acquisition, Franklin Quest decided to sponsor the PGA Senior golf tournament in Salt Lake City. They called it the Franklin Quest Championship Senior PGA Tournament.

Hyrum: "I got to know Jack Nicklaus, Gary Player, Tom Watson, all those guys of that era. But before that time, I didn't play golf. I'd never played golf before. Golf just wasn't my thing. And the first year we had the tournament, my associates asked, 'Why aren't you playing in the Pro-Am?' And I said, 'Hey, you know I don't even know how to play golf. You know I'd probably kill somebody!' So our president, who was a golfer, said, 'Come on, you're embarrassing us. Go learn to play golf!' So, I took my whole family down to Arizona, to the Nicholas Flick Golf School. For three days I think I hit 1,000 balls a day. I mean, I was in traction for a month! What I discovered in those three days was that I could hit a golf ball! So I started playing in the Pro-Am and made some wonderful friends. I was basically dragged into golf kicking and screaming around 1993."

Hyrum Smith and his companies benefited greatly from the seven years of sponsoring those PGA tournaments. He met people who traveled from all parts of the country to play, and he connected with the great golfers of the world. He went on to play with many of the A-listers – the "Who's Who of Golf Royalty!" Hyrum and his wife developed a close friendship with Gary and Vivian Player. In fact, they traveled with the Players to South Africa where Gary Player was somewhat of a celebrity golf legend. They played on three different courses designed by Gary himself! Hyrum recalled, "Traveling with Gary Player in South Africa was like traveling with Queen Elizabeth in England!" He was something of a revered figure among the locals!

Some time after they returned home from South Africa, Gary Player called Hyrum to tell him that Jack Nicklaus was going to honor him at the memorial that year. Gary wanted Hyrum to introduce him at the memorial ceremony. Hyrum happily and eagerly agreed. There were about 2,000 people seated around the 18th green. Hyrum stepped up to the podium and, in his introduction of Gary Player, he told the story of Gary's success. In Hyrum's address to the crowd gathered there, he gave all the credit to Gary's wife, Vivian.

Hyrum: "Vivian is a scratch golfer. She and Gary were childhood sweethearts when they were 16 years old. Vivian's father was a golf pro at a place in South Africa. Gary was the son of a coal miner. He planned to be a coal miner too. That was all he knew. Then, one day, Vivian said to Gary, 'Why don't you try golf?' And the 16-year-old Gary Player said to Vivian, 'What's golf?' So she took Gary over to the golf club where her father was the local pro and said, 'Dad, I want you to teach Gary to play golf.' Well, her father was really ticked off. He wasn't excited about his daughter running around with a coal miner's son. So, he put a two wood in Gary's hand and put a ball on the ground. He said, 'Hit and let's see.' Gary Player had never had a golf club in his hand. He was basically told just to step up there, put his feet wide, and just hit the ball. So, Gary Player steps up to this ball and hits it 260 yards. He had never before had a club in his hand! Vivian's father was totally amazed, and he said, 'Oh, my! You're a hell of a golfer!'"

That's quite a humble beginning for a golfer who went on to win 163 tournaments. Gary Player won the Masters three times; the US Open three times; the British Open three times and the PGA Cham-

pionship twice. At that time, before Tiger Woods rose to fame, he was one of only five players who ever won the four major tournaments. Hyrum learned a valuable life lesson from studying the life and habits of Gary Player.

Hyrum: "You know, one time I was having dinner with Gary, and I asked him how many golf balls he's hit. Gary said, 'I don't know. Nobody ever asked me that.' So, I started to break it down. I asked, 'How many balls do you hit a day?' He replied, 'Well, I hit 500 balls a day.' So, I did the math. Gary Player has hit five million golf balls! Here's my definition of a successful golfer. And you can use this definition in any role you want, but let's use it for a golfer. A successful golfer is willing to do that which the other golfer is not willing to do. That sounds so simple. But Gary Player was willing to hit 500 balls a day. If you're not willing to do that, then don't plan on being the next Gary Player! Similarly, a successful businessperson is willing to do that which the unsuccessful businessperson is not willing to do. A successful salesperson is willing to do that which the unsuccessful salesperson is not willing to do. This applies to the successful father, mother, and so on. This is not rocket science. And so the issue is, if I want to be a golfer, or if I want to be a successful businessperson, I'd better take a long hard look at what successful golfers and successful businesspersons are willing to do. And if I'm not willing to do any of that, then I will have to settle for something far less rewarding."

What makes Hyrum Smith tick? I asked him, "What motivates you to get out of bed every day and give a talk or work on a book?" Where does he get the stamina and desire to keep working so hard every day? In 1963, when he was 19 years old, he went to London on a mission trip with his church. There he had the unique opportunity to hear Winston Churchill speak. Something in Churchill's talk deeply moved Hyrum and has stuck with him ever since. Churchill shared with those in his audience that he felt he had been "called" from very early in his life. He wasn't sure where this feeling came from. But it was instilled in him that he was put on the planet to make a meaningful difference in the lives of others. It was near the end of Churchill's life, and Hyrum remembered Churchill in his speech questioning, "I hope I've made a difference." Hyrum thought, "Are you kidding me? You saved the free world, for crying out loud!" At that moment, at that point in Hyrum's young life, he realized that he, too, was put here for a purpose. And his purpose was, in some way, to make a difference.

Hyrum: "And I keep asking myself, 'Well, have I made a difference yet?' Well, you know I think we made a difference with Franklin. We've touched millions of lives. We've had six million people using Franklin's planner. It grew into a very big company, and we've had offices all over the world. And so, you know I think we've started to make a difference. Now I've started another company based on my book title, *The Three Gaps: Are You Making a Difference?* I am motivated by the feeling that I still have more to do. And so, what gets me out of bed every day is that I'm committed to making a difference and that difference is that I believe I can help bring inner peace into the lives of many people. I can teach them to manage themselves, their lives, and their time better."

Hyrum and I discussed how luck plays into success. Most successful people, at some point in their lives, get a big break. However, that break never comes undeserved. I once heard the expression, "Success is when preparation meets opportunity." I have found this to be true in my own life. I've always felt that preparation plays a big part in getting those lucky breaks. When I work hard on my skills, both on the golf course and off; when I invest my energy in sourcing the most cutting-edge promotional products for my clients; when I conduct research to develop the most effective advertising strategies for my client base; all these things contribute toward my preparation. Then when a very big opportunity comes along, I am prepared for it, and I can take advantage of that opportunity and achieve success. I think Hyrum and I agree that luck plays a part, but luck is definitely not enough.

Robin: "Hyrum, from where did your biggest break come?"

Hyrum: "That's an interesting question, you know. There have been many big breaks. There are lots of things that people call luck, and in many ways, they are luck. But the fact is you had to be there and ready for it when the luck hit. I remember clearly the biggest break that launched Franklin's success. As you know, we had created the Franklin Planner, and we had done a few local seminars here in Utah. I was asked to speak in New York City to a group of IT managers. A guy in Salt Lake City was the IT manager for Inner Mountain Health Care, which is a huge hospital chain here. He was a member of an association of IT managers in New York. They have an annual event in Manhattan, so he convinced them to invite me to speak about time management. I flew to New York, and there were about 85 people in the room. It was really kind of interesting because we wrestled with the idea of giving them all free Franklin Planners. We wrestled with whether we could afford it. Although we really couldn't afford it at the time, we ended up giving them all free planners, and they were quite excited. I gave a two-hour presentation to this group, and I actually got a standing ovation! I didn't think IT people ever gave standing ovations. Well, about four days later, I got a call from the HR director at Dow Chemical in Midland Michigan. He said, 'My IT guy was in New York last week. He saw you speak and thought you were great! We want you to do a pilot seminar here at Dow Chemical.' Then he said, 'If you are as good as these guys say you are, you'll be here a long time. So I flew to Midland Michigan, and we conducted a two-day seminar. There were 55 people in the room, and the response was unbelievable. Over the next eight years, we trained 32,000 people at Dow Chemical. As a result of our success there, we landed Merrill Lynch, where I personally trained 18,000 brokers over an eight-year period. The Franklin Planner just took off! The network of HR directors and training directors in corporate America is very strong. They all know each other. So from there, I heard from Nike, then AT&T, Proctor and Gamble, and it was just amazing. We went from three of us in a basement in 1983 to 4,000 people when we went public in 1992. And we never did any advertising. We called it the breeder effect. It was all word of mouth networking."

This is an excellent example of how being prepared with an audience-tested presentation led to success through a lucky break by way of an opportunity! By being prepared to speak to the group of IT managers in New York, Hyrum was able to make a great impression, which led to viral business growth. It also illustrates how one speech, with 85 high-quality promotional gifts, (in this case the Franklin Planners), ignited the rapid growth of what came to be a very successful public company with 4,000 employees. The successful application of the corporate gift is brilliant here because the planner came with a training program to make sure the recipients used it. Since the planner was something they used every day, it was a daily reminder of the benefits of the Franklin brand. Initially, it was thought that their young business couldn't afford such an expense. But the investment really paid off tremendously –in the massive acquisition of several new Fortune 500 customers.

Hyrum: "It's the best investment we ever made in the whole Franklin experience. That was what really launched us – that event in New York in 1984."

MENTORS AND LESSONS LEARNED

Ask any successful person, and you will find that there are always one or two mentors who instilled in them certain principles, ideas, and work ethic philosophies that were instrumental in their success. Hyrum is no different.

Robin: "Hyrum, as a young person, who did you look up to as a role model to emulate?"

Hyrum: "When I was in England on a church mission, I met a guy named Marion Hanks. He is the one who inspired me to improve my speaking skills. He was one of the most articulate speakers I'd ever had the pleasure to hear. I was only 19 years old at the time, so naturally, I was not very comfortable with the idea of speaking in front of a crowd. In fact, the thought of it was downright frightening. I remember watching this guy speak and thinking how good he was – how he was able to lead and inspire a crowd. I decided that one day I was going to be as good as this guy. I don't think I've achieved that goal just yet, but I continue to make an effort. Of course, my father was the other mentor in my life. He taught me a powerful thing when I was eight years old. It took me 20 years to realize how powerful his words were. He made me memorize this: 'You cannot think any deeper than your vocabulary will allow you to.' And you know, as an eight-year-old, what does that mean? The fact is we think in the words that we know. And Winston Churchill had a working vocabulary of 25,000 words. The average businessperson today has a working vocabulary of about 13,000 words. By the way, there are 340,000 words in the English language. The average American teenager has a working vocabulary of about 2,300 words. In all the studies ever done of successful people, one of the common dominators was a large working vocabulary. They knew their language, and they knew how to use it. I learned very early that the use of the English language is critical to success. That really proved true. Whenever I talk to young people, I tell them, 'You can't think any deeper than your vocabulary will allow you to.'"

Presentation skills are something that we should all strive to continue to improve. Being able to articulate your message eloquently is one of those assets that no one can ever take away from you. It is also a skill that is always useful. No matter what your profession, your success largely depends on your ability to communicate with others. If you can get your message across in a most effective and inspiring way, people will be more likely to respond to your call to action.

THE FRANKLIN PLANNER SUCCESS

Hyrum knew he was on his way to a major success in 1984 when it was time for his customers to decide if they would renew their Franklin Planners. In his business, selling a renewable product is called a continuity program, and the customer retention rate is a measurement of the rate of renewal. It's key to growth. If you can get most of last year's customers to renew for another year, that frees up your resources to sow a whole new crop of customers. A successful continuity program can really cause sales to soar.

Robin: "When did you realize that Franklin Planners was going to be a huge success?"

Hyrum: "We knew we had something very good in the end of 1984. It was time for people to renew their Franklin Planners. Now, remember back then there were no iPods, there were no computers, there were no iPhones, no cell phones and the question we asked ourselves was, 'Gee, I wonder if anybody is going to buy a planner for next year?' It was like the razor blade business. Success depended on the refills! And so, about the first of December, suddenly our phones started ringing, and people were buying their refills. And we thought, 'Oh, man, I think we've got a business here!' It was like lighting a fire that just spread. And at the time, our message to the world was: 'Have everything in one place,' – and that place was your Franklin Planner. When new technology came out, we changed one word of our message. Have everything in one system. That could be your cellphone, your PC, your Franklin Planner, or whatever you happened to be using.

The basic principle of time management hasn't changed for 6,000 years. But the tools we use have changed dramatically."

EMBRACING CHANGE –
GROW WITH THE FLOW

As we can see from Hyrum's account, a necessary component to any successful business is the willingness to embrace change. All too often, we get set in our ways and fearful of doing things differently. This has often been the cause of the demise of many a company, especially in the age of technology. When the personal computer was introduced in the 1980s and became widely used in the following decade, the concept of paper record-keeping and file sharing were on their way out. Those who were afraid of this seemingly "Star Trek-like" technology, rejected the change and were eventually left in the dust, as their skills and communication techniques became obsolete. However, those who would "grow with the flow," benefited greatly from new efficiencies, thanks to automation and technology. Growth through innovation is not only something to be considered but in a winning business, it is continually pursued as a way to make your business more efficient. Work smarter, not harder, for optimum productivity.

STRIKING OUT ON YOUR OWN –
THE ENTREPRENEUR

Many professionals at some point in their lives get that yearning to strike out on their own. Hyrum and I both possess the entrepreneurial experience of the highs and the lows of starting successful businesses. We discussed the enormous potential and payoff as well as the risks that our own start-up endeavors have presented. Hyrum was fortunate to have a supportive boss in the late Frank Lautenberg, former New Jersey Senator and founder of ADP, which went on to become a $10 billion public company providing payroll ser-

vices. Lautenberg told Hyrum, "I understand the entrepreneurial urge. If you've got an urge, you need to scratch it. And if it doesn't work out, you've always got a job at ADP." Now, I'm sure that the founder of ADP didn't extend that offer to all his employees. But he saw something unique in Hyrum. He recognized his talent, commitment, and work ethic. And thankfully, it was not in Lautenberg's nature to hold back such a talented person.

Robin: "What advice would you give a person who is thinking about striking out on his own?"

Hyrum: "For me, I had a pretty nice safety net to fall back on. Frank told me, 'You would be crazy not to do it.' So I broke off and started Franklin, and the rest is history. But, you know the one principle that people need to remember is that they should have a good back up plan. I call it the monkey theory. And the monkey theory says, have a good, firm grasp on the next branch before you let go of the branch behind you. Because if you're in free fall, you've got nothing to save you."

In spite of the risk, Hyrum would encourage a person who has been thinking about starting a business to go for it. In fact, he says even the "slightest inclination to be an entrepreneur" should be pursued. But his encouragement is not without warning: "Make sure that you do your research so that you know what you are getting into." After all, it's the unintended consequences that can often surprise us when we strike out on our own. You will inevitably make mistakes and encounter problems. There will be days when you don't know where your own paycheck is coming from. It's a fact of life to run into challenges when starting and growing a business. But when you're successful, the rewards make all the sweat equity worth your while.

It's how you perceive and address challenges that matters. As an entrepreneur myself, one thing that I've learned along the way is "if you can't fix it, feature it." Believe it or not, there are actually some good problems to have! There are times when a problem can be converted into a fruitful opportunity. The successful entrepreneur will always look critically at a problem and try to identify an opportunity for growth while examining ways to mitigate its negative impacts. It takes courage, it takes heart, and it takes critical analysis to be a successful entrepreneur. But the good news is that these are not rocket science skills. They are usually the skills and lessons learned from the life experience of a hard-working, honest person with a desire to succeed. So, work hard, pay attention, and observe all that you can! For even the smallest, most seemingly mundane matters could contain valuable lessons.

SALES IS NOT A DIRTY WORD

One area of business that can be daunting for many professionals is sales. The thought of selling has the power to paralyze many highly-educated, successful, fully-grown adults in their tracks, preventing them from achieving super-star success! But if you think about it, life is full of selling opportunities, and most people have many more successful sales experiences than they realize. Just to get a non-sales position with a company, we need to sell our own qualifications through a process that usually involves written, oral, and in-person communication skills designed to persuade. That's what selling is! Any time we seek to influence people in our lives to do things they were not otherwise considering, we use sales techniques. Simple things such as convincing a child to eat his vegetables, or persuading a spouse to agree to a particular vacation destination usually require some of the same persuasive techniques used by a seasoned sales pro.

Why do so many get intimidated when they consider the idea of selling as a possible career? Most people are afraid of rejection. That's understandable. It's not pleasant to hear the word "no." Also, many are uncomfortable with the idea of asking for the sale. Some of us have been raised to think asking for something is not polite. Our parents warned us, "Don't ask for it. Wait until it's offered and then you can accept it graciously." This rule of etiquette is proper for cookies and ice cream but can never be successfully applied to sales. Hyrum and I discussed this.

Robin: "We both understand the importance of sales to the successful business formula. Yet we also know that, for many, selling can be a daunting proposition. How would you suggest people get beyond the fear of selling and overcome the unavoidable sales rejection?"

Hyrum: "When a prospect says 'No,' if you think the word *no* in the sales process is the final word, then you're dead in the water. But if you decide when a person says 'no,' what they're really saying is 'I need more information,' then you can still see that sale to a successful close. A 'no' doesn't necessarily mean no. It may mean that they are not ready to make a buying decision. They don't have enough information to say yes just yet. The average person says 'no' to a salesperson six times before they buy. So, when they've said no five times, you should be really excited because only one more time and they're yours! When I was selling automated inventory control for ADP, I was pitching to a major Toyota dealership in the Pacific Northwest. The CEO was very rude, and he was giving me a hard time. When he said no for the fifth time, I jumped out of my seat, and I said, 'Oh, man, I'm so excited. I can't tell you how excited I am!' He said, 'What are you excited for?' I replied, 'Well the average guy says "no" six times before he buys. You just said "no" for the fifth time. You say "no" one more time and you belong to me, my friend!' And you know this guy sat there with a big cigar in his mouth, and he just started laughing. And he said, 'I can't believe you said that.' I replied, 'Hey, you belong to me, man! Just say "no" one more time, and then go ahead and sign my contract.' And he actually did! So, I landed this big Toyota contract because of that theory! The fact is, you can't see rejections as roadblocks. You just have to look at them as learning experiences. If you call it a roadblock, it'll be a roadblock. What a roadblock actually is – is a learning experience. You need to ask yourself, 'Okay, how do I get around, or over this?' It's like golf! You can correlate these selling barriers to golf. It really is a mind game that involves attitude and strategy. If you think you can play golf, you can. If you don't think you can, you can't. And so self-talk is absolutely vital in the business world, just as it is in golf. For example, if I get up there and shank one into the tree, and say, 'Oh crap! I always do that...' that is terrible self-talk. But instead, if I say to myself, 'That's not like me. I don't do that,' then the next time I'll hit one straight down the fairway. In the same way, if you lose a sale or something bad happens in your company, you need to say, 'Hey that's not like us.' But if you say, 'That always happens to us!' then you're dead. That self-defeatist attitude destroys people, and it destroys companies."

Attitude is definitely an essential element to the successful salesperson. Another key factor is having intimate knowledge of the product. A person who knows the product inside and out is equipped to deal with any objection that a prospect may raise. Being equipped with the right answer for every question about a product's features and benefits is crucial to the seamless flow of the sales process. If you have to interrupt the process to go find an answer that you don't readily possess, the prospect will lose faith in you. Since you represent the product, that doesn't bode well for the sale. Another key factor in making a sale is for the salesperson to believe in the product. Whenever possible, the salesperson should also be a customer so that he can provide an effective testimonial. When the salesperson can demonstrate utmost faith in the product by being a loyal customer, it goes a long way toward making a prospect comfortable with the buying decision. Last, but definitely not least, be a business consultant to a prospective customer. Find your prospect's pain point(s). Ask probing questions to uncover the source(s) of the customers' frustrations. When you uncover what ails them, you may have an opportunity to help solve their problems and eliminate their headaches through the use of your products or services. To understand the groups of people who can benefit from your product(s) is to understand your target market.

THE VALUE OF INTEGRITY IN BUSINESS

If you took a group of retiring workers and compared them with a group of brand new workforce members, you would find that those two groups have very little in common. The person entering the workforce today looks very different than the person entering the workforce forty years ago. While young people today may be more technologically savvy, they also lack certain skills and ideals that were common to new members of the workforce in the 70s and 80s. Conversely, while older workforce members are accustomed to certain rewards and benefits of seniority in a company, younger workers realize that they will work for many different companies throughout their careers and not be able to rely on pension guarantees.

Robin: "Having been around the block a few times, how would you characterize the millennial workforce?"

Hyrum: "One of the things that concerns me about the younger workforce today is that you'll find that a lot of young people are not well read. They're just not reading as much as they should. They're spending too much time on their devices and playing their mindless video games. Unfortunately, with all that wasted time, they are forfeiting opportunities to develop valuable communication skills. Earlier, I mentioned the importance of a good vocabulary for success. If they're not reading, they're not developing a good vocabulary.

"In addition, younger people don't know important things like their history. I've found that if you ask young people about the Holocaust, a lot of them don't even know what it was. If you ask why we were in the Vietnam War, they have no idea. They don't understand why or how we got into World War II. Worse than that, what little history they think they know seems to be full of misperceptions. We have a lot of young people now who believe that certain historical figures, such as Harry Truman, were racists or terrorists. There are a lot of opinions out there that seem to have replaced the facts. When a society doesn't know its history, it is doomed to repeat it. When we fail to learn the lessons of history, that is a dangerous thing for the future."

Robin: "What qualities would you look for if you were building a team today?"

Hyrum: "Well, the biggest thing that I look for are people who share my value system. And this isn't a religious thing, but what I have found is that there seems to be a growing lack of integrity in the business world. And if I'm going to build a company, I've got to have people who really value integrity. I built Franklin with a guy named Richard Winwood. We never had a written agreement with each other, and we built a billion-dollar company. The market cap was a billion dollars on Wall Street when we left. We started two other companies together and we never had a written agreement. I loaned him money. He loaned me money, and we would do these things because I knew his word was gold and he knew my word was gold. So in our case, we didn't have to waste time signing papers. That's very unusual, and you can't do that with just anybody until you develop solid trust. The basic idea about what makes companies great in my opinion is having people in those companies who share a good value system. In other words, they have a good work ethic, and they tell the truth. When they tell you they're going to do something, they do it. I've hired many young people. I've recruited from campuses all over the country. What I always look for are good, honorable, solid people. What kind of human beings are they first? And then, oh, by the way, do you have an accounting degree? Yes. Okay, that's a good thing, but you're a good person first – with an accounting degree. And, so the biggest characteristic I look for when hiring is an ethical person of solid character.

"When we went public, a guy by the name of Larry Raider, who was the Chief Analyst from Merrill Lynch came to visit. Merrill Lynch took us public, and Larry came out to Salt Lake and sat in my office for four hours. He was the big guy on Wall Street who decided whether or not Merrill Lynch would take a company public. He never took one note. He never asked for any financials. I thought we were going to have to lay out all our financials. He never asked for them. He just wanted to get to know me. We talked about everything – you name it. And at the end of the four hours, I said, 'Don't you want to see our financials?' He said, 'No, our people can look at your financials later. I'm not interested in that. All I care about is you.' He said, 'Merrill Lynch is going to take you public because of who you are.' I thought that was really interesting. Because normally, in most businesses, they go through your numbers and they go through your company structure. And eventually they did that because they had to create the offering, so they got to know us financially, big time. But making the initial decision as to whether or not they would take us public, they based solely on Larry Raider's recommendation after he had spent four hours with me. So honesty and integrity is not something that you can necessarily detect from a corporate balance sheet. It takes keen insight to get to know a person in a way to judge whether you share the same value system."

Hyrum has such a breadth and depth in his wealth of experience in corporate America. I would have been delinquent as an interviewer had I had not asked him about the most remarkable and rewarding moment of his career:

Hyrum: "You remember in 2001 we had the tragic events of 9-11. Three weeks later, I got a call from Rudy Giuliani's office. We became friends in 1987 when he and I were honored at a banquet together. Anyway, he said, 'Hyrum, we've got a lot of people in pain here in New York. Would you and your partner Stephen Covey be willing to come and do a one-day workshop for the families affected by 9-11?' I replied, 'Absolutely! When do you want us to come?' He said, 'October 19th,' which was five weeks after the attack. He added, 'Hyrum, we can't pay you; we don't have the budget.' I said, 'Hey, no, you don't have to pay us. No worries, we'll be there.' So, Stephen Covey and I flew to New York.

"On the first day, at 5:00 am, Giuliani had arranged for us a tour of Ground Zero, with a police escort. We had to go through four police checkpoints because they had surrounded Ground Zero with 1,600 policemen. You couldn't get anywhere near Ground Zero. And so there we were at 5:30 in the morning, standing on 15 feet of compacted debris. We were looking at this huge hole in the ground, and an NYPD officer who was our escort said he had been there five weeks earlier when the towers fell. He began to recount the horrific details of the events that he witnessed that day. The first-person account of the tragic death and destruction was sobering, to say the least. As he told the story, a three-thousand-degree fire continued to burn, and we watched crews remove rubble and cranes lift beams, dripping molten steel, from the crater. I'll never forget that scene.

"After the tour, we went back to the hotel to shower because we were covered with soot from Ground Zero. Then we went down to the ballroom where there were about 2,300 people crammed in there. Covey and I each spoke for two hours. One thing I said to them, 'If you don't remember a thing I say today, I want you to remember this statement: Pain is inevitable, misery is optional. The fact is that bad things happen to good people.' Meanwhile, people are weeping and just in shock. So, I continued to explain, 'You guys have been through some extremely difficult experiences these past few weeks. It's how you choose to deal with that pain that ultimately defines who you are.' It was a riveting experience. I stayed for several hours afterward and talked to so many hurting people. It was just a life-changing experience to meet all these people who had lost so much and were trying to make some sense out of all this. They were faced with the reality of picking up so many pieces and moving forward, for themselves and their families. So, that experience, getting to know this tremendous group of people who suffered this unthinkable tragedy is one of the highlights that made a lasting impression on me."

Robin: "That story gave me chills. Thank you so much for sharing. You experienced something in that awful tragedy that very few people ever get to see up close and personal – a massive group of devastated people trying to pick up the pieces after a catastrophic life-altering event. I can see why that experience would stick with you forever."

Robin: "Hyrum, how do you want to be remembered?"

Hyrum: "I think one thing to think about is what do you want to have on your epitaph, you know what do you want on your stone? And I think what I want is 'He made a difference.' Yes, that would make me feel great if I had made a difference in somebody's life, then I've been a success on the planet."

Robin: "Well, you certainly have made a difference in the lives of thousands, and you continue to do so with your many thriving ventures! It was such a joy to spend this time together. I really appreciate you sharing these amazing stories with me."

Hyrum: "My pleasure, Robin. The next time I'm out there in Orange County, we need to get together and play some golf!"

Robin: "You got it!!"

BETSY KING
LPGA Hall of Fame Golfer

www.GolfForeAfrica.org

Robin & Golf Legend Betsy King

L PGA legend and Hall of Famer, Betsy King, is one of the top ten women golfers in the world. She played on tour from 1977 to 2005 with an impressive 34 tournament wins, including six majors. Between 1984 and 1989, she won 20 LPGA events, which was more than any other pro golfer during that time. She was the Captain of the U.S. Solheim Cup team in 2007, where she guided her team to victory.

Today, Betsy continues to play on the LPGA senior tour while promoting her own charity, Golf Fore Africa. Understanding the great value golf brings to fundraising for non-profits and having a history of involvement supporting various charitable endeavors, Betsy uses her golf fame as an asset to help connect with potential donors and benefactors to raise money for poor undeveloped countries in Africa. Her commitment is to raise $10 million over the next five years to bring clean water to 200,000 people throughout Zambia. She has personally pledged $1.3 million to help accomplish the goal.

After a 2006 trip where she witnessed the terrible plight of poverty and HIV/AIDS and its devastating effects on the children of Africa, she came home with a burning passion to make a difference in these children's lives and a vision to do so using her gifts and experience in golf. Betsy's desire is to enlist golfers around the world to join the cause by linking her passion for golf to compassion for children.

I spoke with Betsy about golf and her non-profit organization, Golf Fore Africa.

Robin: "Again, thank you for just taking the time to talk to me. Wow. You've had a very impressive golf career. So, are you still playing professionally at all? Are you competing in any of the senior events?"

Betsy: "Yes, I am. I have been. I mean, there isn't much to play in this year. I don't really have a tournament until June in Seattle. After that, there's a Senior Women's Open in July in Chicago at Chicago Golf Club. And then there's the Senior LPGA Championship in October. Those are the only tournaments to play in this year. It's in French Lick, Indiana. It was there last year too. Last year was the first year of the Senior LPGA."

Robin: "That's exciting! So, can you tell me a little bit about the foundation you started in 2007, *Golf Fore Africa*?"

Betsy: "Well, I started, actually, when I was still playing on the LPGA tour. In 2001, we did a project where we were partnering with World Vision to do community development. We raised $250,000 to address needs in a community in Tanzania. So, we raised that money, and I was planning to go to Tanzania that fall. Then 9/11 happened, and all international trips were canceled. So, I didn't make it to Africa at that time but ended up going there in 2006 with World Vision. I was one of 12 women who went on the trip to Kenya, Rwanda, and Zambia to see the effects of poverty and HIV/AIDS, particularly on women and children. I knew very little about the AIDS pandemic at the time, and also, I'd never seen extreme poverty. And so that trip was life-changing because what I witnessed was that poverty and HIV/AIDS had its biggest impact on women and children. About 60% of the HIV cases in Africa are female. At that time, I think there had been about 12 million children orphaned, which means they lost one or both parents from HIV/AIDS.

"We funded different projects. We funded a medical clinic in Rwanda. We did some housing. We did an economic development piece. And then the last two and a half years, we decided to center our efforts on water because, without clean water, it's hard to do much development in a community. For obvious reasons, without clean water, you have poor health. Lack of water causes a number of childhood deaths, and girls, in particular, aren't able to go to school because they're walking for water. And so, it affects the entire family. It's usually women and girls who are tasked with walking for water.

"I'm actually headed back to Africa next month. I'm going to a water conference in Rwanda and then on to Zambia to dedicate some wells. But it's been very rewarding. We just had a *Golf Fore Africa* board meeting this morning. I was very excited by how our event on Monday went and the number of people and golf pros who are supporting us. It was the *Golf Fore Africa* Scottsdale Pro-Am, our LPGA Pro-Am. We had 44 LPGA pros there to play with fans. It was a great day, and I'm fired up to try to get things going and keep things going. The LPGA is in town this week, so I'm headed out there for the next four days."

Robin: "That's awesome that your event was so successful. I was reading in your materials that the container these women use to carry water typically weighs 45 lbs. I also read that they carry it on their heads."

Betsy: "Well, some women carry it on their head. They also might carry it by hand and also have a baby strapped on their back. It kind of varies. And sometimes they're walking more than once a day to the well. They may have to go two or three times because, if you think about it, how much can you do with that amount of water when you're using it for bathing and cooking? And so it's quite time-consuming. So, when you think about not having clean water, you think, number one, of health. But it also kills education, economic opportunity, and time. It's just so time-consuming to have to keep walking for water, so it has a number of negative effects on a community. When you bring clean water to that community, you turn things around rather quickly. Mothers have more time to spend with their kids; girls are able to go to school; the health of the entire village improves, and economic opportunity is created.

"The areas where we focus are rural, so they grow their own food. When they have access to water, they have better crops, so they're eating better. They may have extra crops that they can sell at the market. So, it's a cycle, and you can begin to get out of poverty by just the simple fact of having access to clean water."

Robin: "I was reading that $100 gives two people clean water for a year."

Betsy: "That's actually for a lifetime."

Robin: "Oh, for a lifetime, wow! That's not much to provide lifetime water for two! When you look at it that way, you can see how many people can be helped!"

Robin: "Please tell me how using your fame in golf has helped you to become a successful advocate for the poor in Africa."

Betsy: "Well, I think we all have a circle of influence. It's just that everyone's circle is different. And for me, I played on the tour for 28 years, and in lots of events. In the tournaments that I played in, there was always a Pro-Am to raise money for the charity and for the tournament. So, it was natural for me to say, I've seen how well Pro-Ams can work to raise money. I know how charitable golfers can be. So, we just put those two things together and started hosting golf events to raise money. Since then, we've expanded to do women's luncheons and clinics. But I would say the majority of the people that support us have some connection to the golf world. And that's how it came together."

Robin: "My company, Wearable Imaging, Inc., is now in its 26th year and I can literally say that 80% of my clients are somehow connected through golf, whether it's playing in a charity event or it's someone I play golf with. I'm also involved with a few organizations helping to mentor new women golfers. You don't have to be good. That's what handicaps are for. Don't you agree?"

Betsy: "Well that's how it is for me with *Golf Fore Africa*. That's why I keep playing. I've made tons of connections through golf and continue to play with donors. And the other thing that's really been a blessing for me is I've been involved with mentoring some younger girls, from junior girls to high school to college. Yesterday, I rode around with the Ohio State women's golf team who are here in town. I'm a friend of the coach. Gosh, they were great. They were good players. And one of the girls that I was playing with wants to turn professional when she graduates next year. And so, she was asking me questions about the tour. In the position where I am now, I just love having that opportunity to help younger players. And I just love it. Golf is a great game that way. You just don't have those kinds of connections through other sports to the same extent that you get them through golf."

Robin: "No, I always say, spend five hours with somebody on the golf course, and you'll know whether you want to hire them, do business with them, marry them, I mean, everything, right?"

Betsy: "Right, exactly."

Robin: "So I'm just curious because the tour has changed over the years in so many ways. But what advice would you give to these young girls who come up to you and say, 'I want to turn pro'?"

Betsy: "Number one, I always say stay in school. Get your college degree. It's something you can be proud of, plus it's something you can fall back on."

Robin: "Very good advice."

Betsy: "Jacquelyn is a college student who I was playing with yesterday. She was asking me, what's the hardest challenge as a rookie? I said two things. First, you don't know where you're going each week. You're playing a new golf course in a different city, and it's hard when you don't know the golf courses. You don't know the hotels or the restaurants. So, it's all new. Second is probably time management. That's a big challenge because you have to have time to practice and play. But there are a lot of other responsibilities that go along with that. They'll ask you to make appearances, to go to Pro-Am parties; you want to find time to work out to stay in shape and all those things. So, time management is really a challenge. I think when you turn 18 you're better off going to college, where you have to learn to manage your time anyway. When you're playing a collegiate sport these days, you have to learn how to manage your time, and that's very helpful for when you turn professional."

Robin: "Great advice! During your years of playing, are there any moments that are most memorable, such as a Pro-Am or winning a certain tournament?"

Betsy: "There are several different moments. Obviously, the first win on tour is special. And it was particularly so for me because I played six and a half years before I won. So, at that point, I thought I might not ever win a tournament on the tour. That's why winning the first one was so special. That was in Hawaii at the *Women's Kemper Open*. It was a regular LPGA tournament. And then, winning a major is special. I won at what was the *Dinah Shore* three times. Also having the opportunity to be a part of the *Solheim Cup* team. That probably is the most nerve-wracking event that you're in. You know, when you're representing your country, and you're representing your team, there's just added pressure that you don't feel in a regular tournament. But it's a lot of fun, the camaraderie and just being around the other players. It's just something different than when you show up as an individual in tournaments week in and week out."

Robin: "You have such an amazing professional record! Of all those wins, do any stories stand out?"

Betsy: "I've met a few celebrities over the years and was invited to the White House several times because of the *Solheim Cup*."

Robin: "Wow. Which presidents have you met?

Betsy: "Well, I've met President Bill Clinton and then George W. Bush. They were the two that I met who were in office at the time. I also played golf with Gerald Ford one year at the *Dinah Shore*, and I met George H. W. Bush at a charity fundraising dinner in Houston. We were both posing for pictures. And actually, I've met Donald Trump, too, long before he was president. We played at an event at Trump National in West Palm Beach. We got to stay at *Mar-a-Lago*."

Robin: "Oh, wow! That's such an honor!"

Betsy: "So that was a lot of fun, and it was an event that continued for a couple of years where first place was a million dollars. And so that was fun."

Robin: "Wow, that's very cool. How did you get started in golf? You started when you were nine years old, right? That's something we share in common."

Betsy: "Right. You know, I grew up in Pennsylvania. My parents learned to play golf as adults, and they started my brother and me with lessons at the local club. I was fortunate in that there were other kids playing. There weren't really any girls that I played with. It was mostly boys until I was 14 or 15, and then there were a couple of other girls who played. I think, as a kid, the important thing is that you have someone to play with. I probably wouldn't have gone out there by myself all the time. But if I could go with my brother or other people, it made it a lot of fun, and that's how I learned to play. It's a great way to spend a summer day."

Robin: "Yes, absolutely! What do you say to people who are so intimidated by the game and say, 'I could never play. I'm not good enough.' I'm sure you hear that all the time, right?"

Betsy: "Yes, it's very interesting because there are challenges to learning golf, cost and the time that it takes to play. We live in a society where everything's instantaneous, and people often don't want to devote four or five hours to do something. Also, I think it's a difficult sport, and it takes a little time to learn to play well enough to enjoy it. I think it can be frustrating at first. But to get around those things, there are public courses and group lessons. You can get second-hand equipment. I think to get direction in terms of lessons is very important. If you can learn the correct way when you start, I think you'll get better. And anybody can. It just takes a little time. But I think the people that love the game, it's because it's a challenge, and it gets you into your own little world and not thinking about whatever problems you have. So, you can really get into the golf."

Robin: "Yeah, totally agree."

Betsy: "And it's outside in beautiful places usually, too. And you meet a lot of great people. It's played at a pace where you can talk and have fun. You're not running at full speed where you're not really talking to the other people you're playing with. It's at a nice pace."

Robin: "Absolutely! Last question, Betsy. How do you want to be remembered?"

Betsy: "I would say, golf-wise, that I gave it my all, for sure, and then hopefully, that I helped make the world a better place in a small way. That would make me feel good."

Robin: "I think you're doing amazing things, and I admire you for that. You're giving back, and you're trying to make the world a better place, for sure. Thank you, Betsy."

MICHAEL REES
CA Office Liquidators

www.CaliforniaLiquidators.com

Mike Rees

M ichael Rees is the President of CA Office Liquidators in San Diego. As California's leading office liquidation experts, with over 25 years of experience, they specialize in the full-service liquidation of commercial office equipment. He is also a very active golfer, successfully using it as a tool to make connections and build lasting relationships both professionally and personally. Mike just happens to be happily married to my business coach of six years, Allison Maslan, CEO of Allison Maslan International, a Global Business Mentoring Company. (More about that later in my interview with Mike.) I had the opportunity to sit down and chat with Mike about golf, business, and how a business coach can help launch a career.

Robin: Mike, I know you're in commercial office liquidation, but I'm not sure exactly what that is. Can you give us a 30-second elevator pitch about what it is you do?

Mike: "What I do is, I decommission large facilities. So, when a company is moving, or expanding to a new place or sometimes downsizing or going out of business, I will come in and do an inventory of all their office-related assets such as furniture and fixtures. Then I will make an offer to purchase those assets, which includes breaking it all down and moving it out. We then repurpose those assets for the use of other dealers and businesses around the country. We help determine a project timeline, and cost, and manage the logistical coordination while returning our clients' office spaces back to pre-leased conditions. It's a great way to save businesses money while keeping a lot of junk metal out of the landfills. I have warehouses in Los Angeles, Orange County, and San Diego. I am very fortunate because I really love what I do."

Robin: "Let's talk golf. How did you get started?"

Mike: "I started playing golf probably like most people, playing with the family. I was around ten years old and learned to play with my dad and two brothers. We'd go out, and it was just a good way to have that family experience for five hours out on the course. I learned to play years ago when my family lived in up-state New York. I wouldn't call the place we played a golf course. I'd call it more of a pasture with circles cut into the field. It was a lot of fun, and I was the youngest of the family, having two older brothers. I come from a very competitive family, and that has always driven me to do better. So that's one of the things that I love about golf as well. It's very competitive. You're competitive with yourself, but you can be competitive against others too, especially with a handicap system."

Robin: "What about making business connections through golf? Can you share your experience?"

Mike: "As for networking? Well, in the beginning, I was so involved with the nuts and bolts of starting a business that I didn't have the time. I wish I initially began to network back then. I believe that networking is a word that is often misused. Most people perceive it as meeting with a group of people for the purpose of finding leads to ultimately generate sales. I don't consider networking to successfully happen quite that way. I imagine networking as more of an organic thing; really just connecting with people on an authentic, personal level – relationship building. Eventually, you relate on a business level because you know that person well enough and feel comfortable bringing them into your professional circles.

"Once my business was off the ground, I was motivated to invest more time expanding my network to try and grow my business to the next level. Networking is really just taking your net and casting it wider in order to meet more people. As you get to know these people, and they get to know more about you and your business, you begin to develop friendships and establish mutual trust. Contacts who know and trust you are willing to refer business to you because they know you as a person and they have confidence in your honor and integrity. My business contacts know that they are not risking their professional reputations when they open doors for me by recommending me to their associates. There is mutual trust. That's what most people are looking for in relationships so that when they do take chances and refer people, they don't have regrets. They have to ask, 'Can I trust this person to do a good job for my friend or business associate?' Because it's your reputation on the line when you refer someone if it doesn't work out well. So, networking, for me, is really all about expanding my business contacts and getting to know them better on a personal level. Do they have integrity? Are they honest? Do they walk the walk, and not just talk the talk?"

A LUCRATIVE GOLF CONNECTION

Mike shared with me a story where golf was used as the conduit to establish a business relationship built on solid ground. This particular story illustrates the dramatic impact golf has had on the growth of his business, just as it has for many other successful people.

Robin: "Can you tell about a time you made a connection through golf that turned out to be beneficial for your business?"

Mike "Yes! I a made a connection through golf which led to some very large business deals with a major worldwide electronics company in San Diego. This company has about thirty locations. They have an annual golf tournament. It's actually a scramble golf tournament. I played with one of their top facility managers who was responsible for probably ten or eleven of their locations. He played in their tournament for about 22 years and had never won. There's typically some pretty fierce competition among the players in this particular tournament. So he asked me to play in the foursome with him because he knew I'm a pretty decent golfer. I went out and shot the round of my life. I mean, I was putting at two feet from the hole. I was making eagle putts. And we actually ended up winning the tournament. Finally winning this annual company tournament meant a whole lot to him. To me it was great, but for him, winning this thing for the first time was a thrill. It was a huge deal.

"Well, maybe two to three weeks later, I got a call, and I was presented order after order of these high dollar contracts: $50,000; $75,000; $100,000-dollar jobs! So, because he got to know who I was on the course – who I was as a person, he took me under his wing and entrusted me with these contracts. By playing golf together, he saw first-hand that I was a man of integrity, a man of my word. He knew that I would not only talk the talk but also walk the walk. We developed a great relationship that continues to this day."

CHARACTER AND MOTIVATION

Robin: "Are there times when you play golf with a person and find out things that cause you to avoid engaging in business?"

Mike: "You definitely get to connect with some very good people on the golf course. But yes, unfortunately, at some of these tournaments, there are people who are willing to cheat. But that is important information to know too! A golfer might say, 'Hey, we got a birdie there,' when we only got a par. So, when you see somebody out there dropping a ball that went out of bounds, and playing fast and loose with the score, it's revealing as to their character. How do they accept a win, knowing that they didn't deserve it? If they're willing to do that to win on the course, what will they be willing to do to win off the course, or maybe in business? Playing golf for five hours shows you a lot about who a person is. It's a strong indicator of how that person will conduct business. But it's not just about whether a person is playing the game honestly. It also reveals how a person responds to various challenges and circumstances. A person's true colors really come through when you see him under pressure, or you see how he handles winning and losing. You become more familiar with that person's intellect, his ability to strategize, and his sense of humor – all of which are important criteria when building relationships. There have been times when I've wished I had the opportunity to play golf with people before doing business with them. It may have motivated me to form a beneficial business alliance earlier, or warned me to avoid getting into a less than ideal arrangement. Show me a person's golf game, and I'll show you who that person really is. I'll show you that person's character."

Mike and I discussed his inspiration and what motivates him. He touched on how his business philosophy is a major factor in the successful growth of his company. He also shared some daily inspiration that has helped to keep him grounded while pursuing his goals.

Mike: "My dad, who played golf, was a man of just incredible integrity – I mean unbelievable integrity. I inherited his business sense and his strength in mathematics. So, he is one such motivator. The other place where I found my daily motivation – and this was 25 years ago – was in the book, *Greatest Salesman in the World* by Og Mandino. It's not a 'how-to' sales book *per se*. It's more of an attitude adjustment for a person who earns a living, in part, through sales. The advice really hit home. First, it took me out of the 'sales hat' mode and refocused my priorities to living each day with love in my heart. From there, all good things flow. So for 25 years, I have begun each morning with the affirmation, '*I will greet this day with love in my heart, for this is the greatest secret of success in all measures. Muscles can split a shield and destroy life, but only the unseen power of love can open the hearts of men*.' So for me, starting my day like that, with this inspiration, has been a life-changing practice.

"This attitude has helped me to see that the professional relationship is much more than just a sales transaction. If you're out there trying to meet people without actually getting to know who they are, but just focusing on trying to make a sale, you're missing a lot. People want to buy from people who are authentic. If you're not authentic, people can see right through that. It's just another sales pitch. Sales pitches can really turn people off. I will run fast and far in the other direction if I see a pitch. Why should I expect anyone to treat me any differently? It's about much more than a sales pitch. I consider closing a successful sale as earning trust by building an authentic personal relationship. We become partners in a transaction. Our interests become mutual."

CONNECTING THROUGH GOLF

Robin: "Do you think that golf is one of those things that can be helpful in building an authentic personal relationship?"

Mike: "As I mentioned earlier, golf wasn't involved much in my initial success, except to the extent that my father instilled his values in me, and often he did that through the game. I wish I had an earlier understanding of the power of networking through golf and spending five hours on a course getting to know a person, and of course, the opportunities golf provides in meeting other people. But once I realized how effective golf could be in developing solid relationships, I joined a morning golf group. We played once a month. We'd get together with people from all different industries. I also joined another networking golf group. Some groups have better chemistry than others. Every round, you get paired with a variety of different people. Eventually, after I grew my company to a certain point, I was able to target my audience and initiate my own golf events. I began inviting targeted groups of people to events – those who operate in vertical markets, such as commercial brokers, moving people, and those who provide services which complement mine, such as transfer of voice and data. By surrounding myself with contacts in parallel markets, I was able to zero in on a network of professionals with whom my business had common interests. It was much more effective than the cold networking that results in the random contact with fewer mutual interests."

PUT ME IN, COACH!

As I explained at the beginning of this chapter, I met Mike through his wife, Allison Maslan, who has been my business coach, mentor, and friend for six years. So, I thought it appropriate to ask about the importance of having a mentor or coach in business.

Mike: "As an entrepreneur, whether you're running a six-figure or seven-figure company, or whatever type of business you're running, it's extremely beneficial to have the kind of support that you will get from your business coach. It can get lonely at the top of the organizational chart because, even though you work with so many different people, no one has the complete vision that enabled you to start your business in the first place. No one has the overall responsibility for the outcome either. So you can feel like you're on an island at times because the buck stops with you. You run the show. Every opportunity and every issue stops at your door. So to have that coach; to have that mentor; to have that support system, is critical.

"You might close a big deal, or you might fall on your face. Either way, it's helpful to know you can pick up the phone and there's somebody there. When you were younger, and you needed to share your joy or your pain, it was your mom who you reached out to. In business, you're not going to pick up the phone and call your mom. You need that mentor, someone who understands your business and is interested in your success. You need that coach to give you props when you succeed. You also need that coach to provide support when things aren't going as well as planned. You need the encouragement and the perspective. Sometimes, you need to hear that it wasn't necessarily a failure. It was more of an opportunity to learn something valuable and apply it to the future success of your company. The coach is there to help you get off center and figure out how to work through the complex issues of running a business.

"As an entrepreneur, there are times when you are so isolated. There are times when you feel like you're out there on a lifeboat and nobody is around. It's a lifesaver to have that coach to see things through their eyes; to get a fresh perspective and discover different ways to get you out of the box that you're in. Whether it be finding new revenue streams, or looking at innovative ways of doing business, it's a huge help. After we're in business for several years, it's inevitable to suffer from a bit of tunnel vision. Your coach is there to help broaden that horizon and recognize ways to diversify a product line or identify new markets, or new ways to conduct business or other opportunities for growth.

"The value that the coach has to the business is absolutely huge! And the coach has to be someone who actually has an authentic interest in the success of your business. It's not necessarily about your money, not about your paycheck every month. But the coach must really care about you as a person and your success. It really comes down to the authenticity and the sincerity of that coach. Allison cares so much about her clients and their success, and that's her life's mission, to help people better themselves; to help navigate around the roadblocks that prevent or limit success. Sometimes we set up self-imposed barriers which we can't break through. She helps identify those and take them out so that her clients break through to the next level, which is absolutely huge. She's more excited at the success of her clients than they sometimes are! She has the ability to motivate her clients, and she won't let you give up. She won't let you stop striving to be better."

ROADBLOCKS & ANALYSIS PARALYSIS

Robin: "Mike, while we are on the subject of roadblocks, can you share your successful strategies for navigating past them in life, both professionally and personally?"

Mike: "A roadblock is not something to turn away from. It's not a stop sign. It's more of a yield sign. It's signaling that maybe there is a different way to do things. It challenges us to analyze our options and find an alternative path. Do we need to go around it? Do we need to take the bricks down and go through it? Or put it in four-wheel drive and go over it?"

Mike continued about the similarities between the roadblocks in business and the hazards on the golf course. We encounter them at every hole. In comparison, it's very clear that golf is so often an appropriate metaphor for many aspects of life! It's often a risk versus reward proposition as Mike further explains.

Mike: "You start out on the course, as in business, and things seem to go smoothly at first. And then you get down the road, and inevitably there is a roadblock. Some sort of challenge arises. Suddenly, there's a huge sand trap or a water trap. You have to decide, 'Do I lay up and play it safe with the green right over the water, or do I go for it?' What are the risks of taking a chance versus the rewards of going for it and getting it right? And it often seems to me that the rewards outweigh the risks. Golf is a great analogy to business because you don't go for it all the time. There are times when you play it safe, and other times when your overall chances of success are better. But more importantly, there are times when you just have to lose the fear. Fear can be your biggest roadblock to success if you let it paralyze you. In golf, if you're standing over a ball, and the thought goes through your mind that there's water ahead, you are going to hit the ball into the water. One hundred percent of the time, you will hit it in the water if you let the fear be the focus.

"It's amazing the way the mind works. If you try and take the fear out of it, you are free to perform like a pro and the sky is the limit as far as what you can achieve. One thing about golf for me is that I can be free to take some chances on the course. I play so much better under pressure. But I've seen some golfers absolutely fall apart under pressure. It's interesting to see how people fold like a crate when the big shot is on the line. I can see it in their eyes standing over the ball. There is that lack of confidence in the shot. They're thinking too much. You have to take the brain out of the game, don't overthink, and just go for it!

"Sometimes it's the same with business and in life. You can overthink things, or you can continue to delay, waiting for everything to be perfect before you make that big decision or take that shot. Sometimes you need to jump in with both feet and go after the big rewards. The rewards don't come without making a major commitment to take the business to the next level. And fear is, without a doubt, our biggest roadblock in business, just as it is in golf. People can be so paralyzed by indecision because of fear. They avoid making big decisions because they're fearful of a negative outcome. What about the positive outcome of when it goes right? And so it's like that with golf. If I focus on the fear, I will set myself up for failure. But if I focus on the success and take the fear out of the equation, I have a greater chance of achieving success."

I have wondered myself if the "fear of failure" for some is actually a "fear of success" in disguise. I've observed in business that people sometimes sabotage their chances of success without even being aware that they are doing it. Is it because if they succeed, more will be expected of them? When you are overwhelmed with the idea of failure or success, it's helpful to consider your worst-case scenario. In doing so, one can usually dispel most fears because the worst thing that can happen is usually not so bad. It's also important to understand your own risk threshold. What is it that I'm willing to

risk? And like golf, it is really understanding the risk/reward propo-
sition that separates the winners from the losers.

Mike and I decided that being very risk averse sometimes stems
from analysis-paralysis. When a person overanalyzes a situation, it
can get to a point when they become incapable of making any deci-
sion at all. That's when it becomes self-sabotaging. In that case, what
a person might really be doing is avoiding a decision altogether, out
of fear. And sometimes, that's okay! Mike illustrated this concept
humorously.

Mike: "My wife Allison makes fun of me because I can go
into a six-story high rise building in downtown L.A., walk through
six floors full of cubicles and fixtures, and make a decision about
whether to take on this massive job in about ten minutes. But if I
go into a TGI Fridays and look at their menu, I cannot make a
decision about what to have for lunch!"

Robin: "Well, there are only about 25 pages in that menu!!
And it's okay to suffer from analysis-paralysis over a decision
about lunch because there's not much at stake. But when it comes
to decisions in business, similar to golf, you have to live in the
moment. Obviously, when you know your business, just as you
know your golf game, it's easier to make those time-sensitive decisions under pressure. Experience cannot be undervalued in
such a situation. But it's definitely crucial to understand when you
are delaying a decision for reasonable purposes or because fear
has you paralyzed. And I can't place enough emphasis on knowing your business like the back of your hand. Because when you
have the knowledge and experience, it's easier to weigh the pros
and cons, and the decisions almost make themselves."

"Mike, I really enjoyed chatting with you about golf and especially the way you applied the lessons of golf to life and business.
Golf can be a metaphor for so many things! It's been a while since

we played. We definitely need to set up some tee time, soon! My final question for you is, 'How do you want to be remembered?'"

Mike: "I don't want to think about that stuff, to be honest. I never thought I'd get to this point in life after my crazy childhood! But seriously, if somebody is talking about me at my funeral, I would be happy to be remembered as a person who lived life with passion and zest, and as someone who cared a lot about others. I want to be remembered as a great husband who loved his wife – an authentic person who could be counted on, who would be there in times of need – without judgment. I want to be remembered as a person people just loved to be around. As we get older, we realize what's important in life. Growing up, I knew people who were so negative that I hated to be around them. Then I knew others who were an absolute joy to be around! I want to be remembered as a person whom people loved to spend time with because I had a joyful passion for life. We don't leave this life with a lot. What we leave with is our family name and who we are. And you've got to protect that. You've got to leave that clean for your kids, for your posterity."

DONNA HOFFMAN
Women On Course

www.WomenOnCourse.com

Robin with Donna Hoffman

*D*onna *Hoffman is the founder of* Events19 *and* Women on Course. *Established in 2005,* Women on Course, *is the fastest growing women's golf community, helping women golfers feel comfortable and confident participating in the golf lifestyle. Donna inspires women across the country to use golf as a vehicle for business and social networking. Her organization provides easy access to activities and skills that complement women's careers and social lives. From golf outings to wine tastings, travel experiences and style guidance, they remove the intimidation, helping to make women's golf more enjoyable. Donna's talent as an experiential event marketer and motivational leader has been instrumental in growing a large community of dynamic and influential women attracting financial and luxury brand partners.*

Robin: "Thank you so much for spending time with me, Donna. I've heard so much about you and your organization, and I'm very excited to talk to you. So first, what got you started in golf and how do you feel that it's contributed to your success in business?"

Donna: "Well, to answer how I got started in golf, I was not a golfer growing up. I played other sports. I was not introduced to golf until my mid-40s when I was dating. Prior to that, I was married to an avid golfer and golf was his thing. It was something he would do on the weekends. So later in life, when I was dating, I swore off anybody who was interested in golf because I didn't want to be a golf widow. Later, when I was dating, a man introduced me to golf in a very engaging way. Knowing that I really love exercising and being outdoors, he brought me into the game in a way that appealed to the things that I already liked. He took me out on a date to the driving range to hit some balls. It was a gorgeous day and perfect weather. We hit some balls, and then he had a glass of chardonnay waiting for me. It was the perfect date. It turned out that I really had a knack for it and I liked golf, and that's how I got my start in the game.

"Now I'll answer your second question regarding how golf has contributed to my success in business. I sold my company to a very large defense contractor. They retained my services for a period of three years. So, I was wondering what I was going to do at the end of the term. After 18 years in television production, I had no idea what my next career was going to be. When I started getting passionate about golf, I thought, 'Wow, this is a really cool environment and lifestyle. More women need to know about this!' That's when I came up with an idea to produce a television show about the golf lifestyle. So, golf helped me by giving me my next career move. I took that television show, which became a couple of happy hour events to bring women together who like golf, and from there, all the dominoes fell into place. A sponsor appeared, other key players appeared, and next thing you know, I had started a company called *Women on Course*. The mission was all about helping women get into the game and helping them make connections with other women golfers."

Robin: "Very cool. Can you share any stories where golf was the connector in a successful business transaction?"

Donna: "One of the things that happened when I was producing a television show about golf resulted in a big break for me. Our office was in the corporate headquarters of the defense contractor that bought my company. There were about 2,000 people on site. Our little unit consisted of only about ten people. Up until that point, I had never met anyone in the company. We were our own video production unit. One day, I accidentally left some materials about the golf show on the copier. Someone came to find me, and he happened to be the head VP of contracting. He was very interested in the materials I had left behind, and he wanted to learn what I was doing with golf. So there I was with this very high-ranking person in the company, and we were talking about their corporate defense contracts and my video production services. They happened to be bidding on a project that had a video component to it and were planning to outsource the video production part of the project. They had no idea that the capability existed in-house. We worked out a deal and became part of their bid. They won the contract, and we got a huge video subcontracting job out of it, all because I left something on the copier about a golf show. So that connection didn't even happen on the golf course!"

Robin: "That's awesome. Even indirectly, golf has the potential to connect people to deals! From where do you get your inspiration? Is there anyone in particular to whom you attribute some of your initial success?"

Donna: "I get a lot of inspiration from my father. He's still conducting business at the age of 84. He has been an entrepreneur and a very positive person. He's proud of saying, 'I was born happy.' He was born in the middle of New York, and not of a wealthy family. He went to college on a basketball scholarship. In fact, he didn't know anything about college; he just showed up there with a valise in his hands. There is a lot of wisdom in his sense of humor. He often says, 'Business is just like sports, except you just use money to keep score.' He believes there's always a solution, there's always an answer, there's always an idea. He always tells me, 'Chase your dreams!' And he's done that for himself. My mom passed away a few years ago, and he said, 'All right, I grieved. I'm going to find someone.' And he set his mind to it. At 82, he went out and found what he was looking for in a woman, and they got married. He's so happy.

"My father is fond of saying, 'You can do anything!' I think a lot of women suffer from insecurity or indecisiveness. Some are not so fearless. I'm 58 years old. During my youth, girls weren't generally encouraged to follow their dreams as readily as they are today. They were raised to believe that women might not be able to do certain things. I think that since I'm the oldest child of my family, and my dad didn't have a son first, he just poured all his encouraging philosophy into me. And still to this day, if I'm faltering or I don't know what to do, he is my biggest supporter. He's done it all himself. He's very inspiring."

A NON-NETWORKING NETWORKER

Robin: "How instrumental was networking to your original success? Or was it?"

Donna: "I don't consider myself a networker in the classic sense. I don't go out and actively network. However, I told everyone in my close circle of contacts: family, friends, co-workers, that I'd like to take this golf thing and make it a business. From that, the networkers among those in my circle introduced me to amazing people. That's how I was introduced to *USA Today Newspaper* and a guy who ran a sports marketing company. This coworker that we hired to help do the television show told me, 'You need to meet somebody.' She introduced me to a man who said, 'We could take this little happy hour thing and make it into a huge, national business. I know just the people to bring in.' He brought in *USA Today.* They paid me some money to keep it going while they looked for sponsors. I don't know if you call that networking, but that is how I met those who were instrumental in launching this business. After five or six years, everything runs its course, and we were back to needing a new big sponsor. Without a sponsor, you really can't run this business. I said, 'I've got to find another source of income. Sell it, partner, I don't know.' Once again, I began telling everyone in my closest circles. The next thing you know, I met with the people at Billy Casper Golf, which is a national golf course management company, named for the late, great golfer of the same name. I had one meeting with them, and they said, 'We want to partner with you.' So again, for me, it has been expressing my intentions to my close network of people. Those people have the big Rolodexes, and the ability to connect the dots. So my intentions rippled out to places where the connections were made."

Donna asserted that she doesn't consider herself a networker. Yet, she described in the very next sentence a classic networking strategy. Often people avoid the word "networking" because, for some, it has a negative connotation – like a cold-call sales pitch. But a good networker would never burn contacts. Actually, Donna is a very good networker because, in the next sentence, she described how she naturally communicated with all the people in her life about her project, desire, goals, and dreams. By sharing this aspirational information with people with whom she naturally communicates, she started the networking ball rolling. They kept her goals in mind and connected her to people who had the resources to help get her venture off the ground. The best networking happens in that organic, unforced, subtle way. If you feel like you are interrupting and unwelcome, you probably are. The skilled and effective networker is a person who builds strong relationships first. Then, it is through these authentic alliances that the valuable connections are effectively made. As we discussed further, Donna illustrated how her successful brand of making connections was instrumental to the success of her venture, Women on Course:

Donna: "When I did the television show, there seemed to be a great deal of interest in golf among women. Many were asking, 'How do I get into the game of golf? What do I do?' It seemed that everyone wanted to golf, and I thought, 'What do I do with all of this interest?' One of my friends said, 'Let's get a bunch of people in Washington, D.C. who play golf and we'll have a happy hour at a local restaurant, *Flemings*. There we can brainstorm and come up with some ideas.' She knew the owner of the establishment and could arrange it. I said, 'Okay, that sounds good.' I'm an entrepreneur, so I'm always trying to find ways to turn an opportunity into a business. After that happy hour, a few things happened. The ladies had so much fun, loved meeting everyone, and wanted to do it again. And the owners of Flemings said, 'This is great! You brought all of these executive businesswomen into our restaurant. We're new here. They didn't know about us, so we'd like to do this again, and we'd like to do this at other locations. You could plan these happy hours, and we'll help you turn these events into a business.' That answered the question, 'What am I going to do next?' This was to be my next career.

"From that point on, I provided a constant stream of goods, services, and activities to this group of women based on their interests. They wanted to travel, so we came up with golf trips. They wanted to join a club, so we came up with a membership. When Calloway became a sponsor, they offered products for their sponsorship. So every member got a free pair of golf shoes, which caused the membership to skyrocket."

WHERE DO YOU TURN FOR HELP?

Robin: "Do you feel it's important to have a business coach or mentor or do you have one yourself, personally?"

Donna: "I don't have a business coach in the formal sense. But I do have a few people who help me in the brainstorming process. I think it's extremely important to have somebody mentoring you, coaching you, and supporting you. Doing it alone, as a solo person, is hard. And I'm saying that as a pretty strong person as far as business goes. But sometimes you have doubts. You might question yourself. To keep things moving along, I think it's very important to have somebody on the sidelines to cheer you on."

Not everyone has access to the benefits that a formal business coach relationship can bring. But as an entrepreneur who has retained the services of a business coach over the past six years, I can attest to the effectiveness of such a partnership. Since developing an alliance with my business coach, my sales have increased TEN-FOLD. I would recommend to any entrepreneur who is serious about being successful to engage these services if possible. If not, find a trusted advisor in a retired sage, or some other experienced guru from whom you can seek wisdom and guidance on a regular basis. Earlier in my entrepreneurial career, I had my dad, and then Bud Gordon, both older men who I could lean on for business advice. The key is to have regular discussions in order to keep goals on track.

NAVIGATING THROUGH ROADBLOCKS

Robin: "What are some of your successful strategies for getting around roadblocks in life, either professionally or personally?"

Donna: "Well, one of my strategies is new. When I hit a roadblock that I can't seem to get around, and I feel stressed or panicked, I've learned from experience that it's usually not the best time to make a difficult decision. It's probably okay to table something for a day or two, and you don't have to make a decision right there on the spot. Not having to rush into a decision and doing it on my timetable has helped me a lot. Also, I have a very solid work ethic. I like to get things done. When I hit a roadblock, I have found that sometimes you need to take a break. I have some guilty pleasures. And sometimes I need to step away from the stress of the problem for a few hours. Golf is a great way to clear your head. You're so focused on the game that you forget every problem in the world. When you come back, you are fresh to face your challenges with renewed energy and a fresh perspective. Something that seemed impossible before may be an easier challenge to meet after some time away. If that strategy doesn't work, I can usually find resolution through a combination of advice from trusted confidants and outsourcing parts of the problem to those more qualified to deal with it."

Like everything in life, knowledge is power. If you want to be successful, you better know what you're doing. And while knowledge is important, it's sometimes even more important to <u>know what you don't know</u>. The person who thinks he can be all things to all people will eventually disappoint. So, if you want to be successful in business, you have to know when it's time to call in the professionals. I often tell myself, 'Stay in your lane, Robin.' That's hard to do, especially for an entrepreneur. We tend to embrace challenges and want to find all the answers ourselves. But with so much that needs to get done, you have to learn how to delegate efficiently if you want to run a successful business.

WOMEN ON COURSE FOR THE BEGINNER

Robin: "Can you talk to me about how you teach women non-golfers to get out on the golf course and play? What is the format of your program?"

Donna: "Yes, we have the 'never touched a golf club' group. I break it down into a prepare, practice, and play plan that will get women ready to play on a golf course. At the event, I spend an hour with an overview of the game – the object, parts of a golf course, how the score works, and then we move on to what to wear and bring to play the game. Next, we tour the club and walk through how to check in, get a cart, and head out to the course where I play a hole. We go over some basic etiquette and how to manage when you are not a skilled golfer. After that overview, the women move to the practice range for some hands-on instruction. This is very popular, and it's a fun way to be introduced to the game, especially in the company of ten or more women."

Robin: "Before our interview, you mentioned that because you work with a lot of novice golfers, you have some funny stories. Can you share some of these about teaching golf to beginners?"

Donna: "I usually work with the group of women who have never touched a club in their lives. The questions that they ask me are so funny. One time we were out in San Diego on a golf course and I had about twenty ladies. I usually take them on the hole and I explain the game by playing a golf ball. We were waiting to tee off at the forward tees, and one lady asked about the tee markers, 'Are those little balls Bocce balls, so while you're waiting for your tee shot you can play a game of Bocce?'"

Robin: "That's great!!"

Donna: "Another time I was sharing the concept of hitting a bucket of balls at the driving range. I explained to this group of ladies, 'You go to the pro shop and buy a bucket of balls, and then you go out on the range and practice hitting the balls.' One lady came to me later and asked, 'Donna, I bought the balls like you said, and I hit them all out there, but how do I get them back?' She bought a brand-new box of golf balls and hit them all out there. She didn't hit the range balls. I think we should change the lingo now to 'renting a bucket of balls.'"

Robin: "These are really funny stories. Having played golf for about 50 years, I don't even remember not knowing the basics. I love that these people are innocent and don't understand. You need to write these stories down! Just share them in a blog or something. That would be fabulous! Do you have another one?"

Donna: "When I take them on their golf tour, the first place we stop is at the starter. I explain that the starter is responsible for controlling the pace of the game. He provides relevant course information and calls on the players to begin at the first tee at the appropriate times. Before I bring the ladies out, I make it a point to warn the starter, 'Okay, I'm bringing these ladies out. Tell them what you do and remember, they don't know golf.' When he was finished explaining everything, I asked the ladies, 'Does anyone understand what he said?' They all replied, 'No, we have no idea what he was talking about,' even after I prefaced it by saying, 'They don't know anything about golf, so please speak in a language they'll understand.' I still had to translate what the starter said.

"Another common funny thing that happens with new golfers, I'll say 'Everyone grab your putter, come on we're going to putt.' Out of ten people, usually four of them bring their pitching wedge because they see the 'P' and don't know the 'P' is for pitching wedge."

Robin: "Seriously, you need to start a blog! These are great!"

Donna: "This one is funny. I had a new beginner golf group and all eight of us were out there. I asked, 'Who would like to hit the tee shot?' One girl volunteered, 'I'll do it.' When she got up to the tee, everyone stopped talking. She turned around and asked, 'Why have you all stopped talking? The quiet is making me nervous! Talk, keep talking!' She didn't know that was etiquette. It's really fun; I really love teaching the beginners all about golf. It brings me so much enjoyment."

Robin: "You and I have been playing golf for a long time, so we take these things for granted – but it really must seem weird if you don't know the lingo and the etiquette. That's probably why some people are reluctant to do it. That's where *Women on Course* can really help the beginner. Golf has a unique culture and language. And you provide the cultural and language translation."

86

WOMEN ON COURSE – DIFFERENT STROKES FOR DIFFERENT FOLKS

Donna: "I think one of the reasons ladies like *Women on Course* is on the Signature Golf Experience, we put you in the right group. That's where our ambassadors come in handy to really help set the stage. We communicate with our members, 'This is for course-ready and above players.' 'This is for new and learning players,' so members get the appropriate amount of instruction.

"We implemented these skill level distinctions because of a few problems we experienced earlier – this happened in one of our chapters. I have a group of ladies who play all the time. They all have handicaps, and they called me from the course. They said, 'Donna, there's this woman that showed up, and she's taking the wrapping paper off her clubs.' I said, 'I don't understand.' The reply came back, 'She just bought the clubs; she's a new golfer. What are we going to do with her?' This woman who was brand new to golf signed up to play 18 holes, and she went and bought clubs the night before. Clearly, she wasn't prepared to play 18 holes. I didn't want to put them in the position of having to teach a brand new golfer. Yet, I didn't want to insult the beginner. She was a partner of a big consulting firm."

Robin: "Right, so you can't just tell the group of women, 'Oh, you have to help her along and teach her how to play golf.' And you also can't discourage the woman who showed up with the new clubs, eager to play. That must have been a tricky situation."

Donna: "I can't remember how that situation played out. But it definitely motivated me to make some changes. When I reinvented *Women on Course*, one of the areas that I addressed was setting expectations so that each golfer is assigned to a skill level appropriate to her experience. Experienced golfers can act as ambassadors, if necessary. That person is trained to handle these kinds of unusual situations. If someone like the woman with the clubs showed up today, she would have been assigned to an ambassador, who might say, 'Look, this is probably not for you. Why don't you ride with me, I'll help you through, but you're going to pick up the ball and move it around.' Identifying the levels has helped to avoid having people participate at the wrong level."

I wanted to interject here that I personally love it when I play with a group of ladies who are at a lower level, and they ask me for help. They see me hit a ball and they say, 'Wow, if there's anything you can do to help or any tips you can provide, please do.' I love when people are open to improving their skills. I know for myself, if there's something I'm not good at, I'm always asking those more skilled than I for suggestions. I'll say, 'Just tell me whatever you need to tell me.' I'm very appreciative of the patient person who takes an interest in helping me to improve my skill. Sometimes, it's just small etiquette stuff like, 'Okay, when you're on the putting green, you don't ever want to walk in somebody's line. You always want to walk around.' Or, 'You always want to make sure the pin is taken out when you're on the green.' These little tips are usually very much appreciated. But I typically don't like to offer that help unless people ask upfront. If you are new to golf, keep this in mind and, if you find someone who you think would be receptive to providing guidance, ask for it! If you are a great golfer, and you see someone struggle, offer a tip! In the long run, this benefits all of us.

Robin: "Donna, can you explain to me these events where you are taking these women out on the course and showing them the very basics of golf? What are these events called?"

Donna: "That's what we call the *Signature Golf Experience*. It's a big event with about 50-60 participants and we choose the nine holes. Some people do the clinic and four holes and some just do the orientation to the game and the clinic. I provide the orientation. I have also given the orientation at tournaments. People have hired me to do that when they have an 18-hole tournament, and they have many people who can't play because they don't understand the game. I'll come into the clubhouse and do this talk for an hour. I'll talk about etiquette, the basics of the game, and tell stories about many of the things I've witnessed over the years. It's a very positive thing!

"I've worked with lots of members, lots of market leaders, and they're avid golfers with handicaps. Some don't seem to understand that people play golf at different levels and for different reasons. The serious golfer plays consistently for score, but there are others who only play maybe once every two years. They need a basic level of knowledge to get out there and feel comfortable. They don't understand when the serious golfer talks over their heads. So, it's helpful to the occasional golfer to be able to have more than a basic understanding so that when they get out there, they can communicate and network with other golfers. There is value in getting up to speed on the basics – enough to consider yourself a golfer. It's funny. I'll ask a group of beginner golfers, 'How many of you consider yourself a golfer?' Not a lot of hands go up. Then I'll explain, 'you are all golfers now. It's just the adjective we're going to put in front of that word. You can say I'm a new and learning golfer or I'm an avid golfer, but you're a golfer.' You may not have a handicap and understand all there is to know. But you have to start somewhere. And many stay at the amateur level for quite some time because they don't go out often enough to progress to the next level. That's okay too! The idea is to bring more to the sport through knowledge while removing the barriers that intimidate and keep people from playing."

Robin: "Donna, it's really been such a pleasure talking with you. You are doing great things for women and golf. I think your mission should be to get a million women playing golf. That would be an awesome legacy! This brings me to my last question: How do you want to be remembered?"

Donna: "That's a great question! I want to be remembered as a person who was positive, helpful, and just someone people wanted to be around, who they could reach out to for help or support. I want to be thought of as a person who got things done and impacted others in a positive way by helping them to be happy with themselves. More specifically, I want to be the person who did all this by introducing, on a massive scale, this fabulous lifestyle called golf."

Robin: "You already are doing these things! I was so excited to learn about your organization through our mutual contact. Obviously, that's how we got connected, and there you go. Proof, once again, that golf is the connector. It's funny. I'm sitting here talking to you about golf, and I'm smiling. Golf makes me smile."

Donna: "I know. I'm smiling too."

ROBERT FORT
Information Technology Executive

https://www.linkedin.com/in/robertfort/

Robert Fort

Robert Fort has been in the information technology profession for some thirty-five years. He has worked in positions from computer services and programming all the way up to CIO – the top technology position on the corporate organizational chart. Robert has been employed in a range of industries including airfreight, consumer packaged goods, entertainment, and retail. In addition, Robert describes himself as a "golf enthusiast," since he took up the sport two decades ago. I had an opportunity to speak to Robert about golf, his successful IT management career, and more.

Robin: "Thanks so much for taking the time to meet with me, Robert. I really appreciate your sharing some golf and corporate management insight. It sounds like you had an interesting climb to the upper levels of senior management. Can you tell me a little about your journey?"

Robert: "Sure. I started out in computer services, then learned programming languages, and kept growing into more responsibility until I had worked my way up to the executive level. Growing up in L.A., it's common to find yourself in the entertainment industry. I've worked with MGM, United Artists, and A&M records, which was a fantastic time. Then I got into the consumer-packaged goods with Nestle and also did some consulting work. I started in the retail industry at Virgin Entertainment and remained in retail for some 15 years. It's a vertically integrated industry, so all of the things that I've learned in all the other positions started to come together. In retail, you get a better view of the bigger picture. You're not just backroom, but you're actually front and center, dealing with the customer. So this was a very good fit for me because one of my skill sets is that I am a big picture person. In the early days, first as a computer operator and then in several other positions along the way, I always asked myself, 'Why are we doing this? What does this mean? How can technology be applied across the entire organization for the benefit of the big picture?' I believe it was that curiosity that helped me to keep moving ahead in my career."

Robin: "So, when did you start playing golf and how did you get introduced to the game?"

Robert: "I started playing golf in the late 1990s. For the longest time, I thought golf was an absolutely boring game. Then, at some point, I gradually became aware of its social value in the world of business. I started working at a company called, Koo Koo Roo, a restaurant chain headquartered here in Los Angeles. There were two guys who were our regional vice presidents and basically ran our stores. They loved to play golf. These two guys took me under their wings and provided me the opportunity to learn to play golf, specifically by including me when they played. At one point early on, they invited me to a golf week in Palm Springs. I said, 'Okay, but I don't play very well.' They didn't mind. They brought me along and drew me into the social part of it. It was a lot of fun. That first day, we played a golf course in Palm Springs, and after 18 holes in 35-mile-per-hour winds, I was pretty worn out. The second day I hit four palm trees – and I had the great distinction of receiving a plaque, (which was really just an award created on a napkin), for hitting four palm trees. These guys thought it was so funny that I hit not just one, but four palm trees in one game. Both of these guys were very supportive, but one was particularly patient and encouraging. Each time I hit a palm tree, he would reassure me saying things like, 'At least the ball went forward!' There was definitely a camaraderie and being included in their golf outings made it so much easier to learn to play in a friendly environment."

Like most avid golfers, after spending some time on the course, Robert fell in love with the game. Now it's more than a recreational activity; it's become somewhat of a lifestyle for him.

Robert: "Early on, there was a moment when I realized I would be playing golf for a long time to come. I was with a friend I knew from church. He would take me to this little three-hole, par-three course over in Sunland. He was teaching me to perfect my swing. I remember one day on one of the holes taking a 7-iron and hitting the ball and getting that perfect ping and watching that ball land on the green, which is the expectation of a par-three like that. I looked at my friend and said, 'That shot just cost me a fortune.' Looking confused, he asked, 'What do you mean?' I replied, 'With that shot, I just became addicted to golf! I remember that moment like I remember the moment of my kids' births."

Robin: "I totally understand that feeling. So how did playing golf help you make connections that were beneficial in business?"

Robert: "Before I learned to play golf, I attended professional conferences all the time, and they usually had golf outings. And so, learning to play finally gave me the confidence to begin going on those business golf outings at the conferences. Golf created these networking opportunities to meet people I probably wouldn't have had the opportunity to get to know. In my case, as the CIO, I'm the guy with the wallet. And there are constantly vendors around who are looking to have conversations with me and try to get a little of that money. So, participating in the golf outings gave me a new way of associating with others in my industry. I've never done a deal on a golf course. I've never done an actual transaction. But I have spent a lot of time on the golf course building lasting relationships. Then, at some point later, I've found myself thinking, 'I know a guy or a lady I could call who would be a good fit for that.' So, I absolutely believe in the power of networking and golf is a great space to begin that. It's been very beneficial along the way, for sure."

Robin: "Were you able to land any jobs or get any consulting work by networking through golf?"

Robert: "It's actually amazing how I've gotten paired up with influential people at these golf events at the professional conferences. There is a lot of time to have these conversations and get to know one another. At times, between jobs or clients, I've been asked, 'What are you looking for? Are you willing to relocate?' And the next thing you know, I'm getting leads. At one point, I was doing consulting work and looking for a full-time position. I was at a charity golf tournament, and on the 16th hole, I got a phone call from this guy. I'm not sure why I took the call on the golf course, but I did. He was calling me to tell me of a CIO opening at a major retail company. I ultimately ended up taking the position."

Robin: "So, what about hiring other people? Is golf a good way to find talent when you're building your team?"

Robert: "One of the biggest problems in IT is finding good talent. A lot of times, I'll be hanging out with fellow CIOs, and I'll learn information that leads me to those resources. One major organization I know was closing, and as they were winding down, their people were starting to disperse and beginning to look for jobs. I was made aware of these available resources through those discussions on the golf course. Again, it points to the networking value of golf."

Robin: "I've always said, 'If you want to get to know a person's character, the best way is to go play golf with them.' Would you agree?"

Robert: "I completely agree with your statement, that you learn about a person's character by playing golf. As I play with others, one of the key things that I learn about is their character. For example, I've played golf with many people who use the foot wedge."

For those of you reading this who are not familiar with the expression, "foot wedge," it is slang for cheating. A person using the "foot wedge" essentially kicks the golf ball to a more favorable position when nobody is looking. Yes, unfortunately, there are people who cheat in golf. At charity golf events, I am often selected the captain of my foursome. I always lay down the law with my team before we play. I say: "I'm just letting you guys know that we are not going to cheat. So, if you want to cheat, find another foursome. I don't need a trophy that bad, okay?"

Robert: "In a positive experience, I was playing an event last year in this recording industry golf tournament. It was a charity providing music programs to inner-city youth. So, I bought extra mulligans, mostly because it was going to this charity. One of those mulligans came into play on the last hole when I had ridiculously putted too hard, and the ball went racing past the hole and missed. This young kid playing with us had driven the green. And here we were walking away with a par. I said, 'Wait a minute, I've got one more mulligan!' I went back up on the green, put the ball down, and hit it. It was about a 35-foot downhill putt and it went right in the hole. We screamed and we ended up winning the whole tournament by one stroke. And that was our last hole. When we were done, we went back and asked each other, 'When did you use your mulligans?' And I just love that feeling knowing that the people I'm playing with are honest. And I was proud that whether we won or lost, even though we had no idea of our standing at that point, the team I was on was totally honest. Unfortunately, I've played many of those best ball tournaments when somebody comes away with nineteen under and I think, really? How is that possible?"

Robin: "Yes, exactly! I've said that so many times – 'Are you kidding me? How is this possible?' Fair play is so important to me. I can't understand why anyone would enjoy golf if they had to cheat to win."

Robert: "And then I've played with others who think it's not a big deal. They say, 'Everybody else is cheating.' And I say, 'No, that's not my heart,' you know? It's the integrity of it that matters to me.'"

That's not my heart – I love that Robert said that because I completely agree with that sentiment. You can definitely tell a lot about a person by engaging them in a round of golf. I find the game of golf to be very revealing as to a person's character. You can learn a lot about a person by their reaction to disappointments and achievements. The way a person responds to the successes and failures of opponents or even team members. Are they consoling? Do they gloat? In life, character really matters. And if a person is willing to win at any cost, even the cost of honesty and integrity, they are likely to have lower standards in other areas of life too. I used to play this course in Arcadia. On the back of the scorecard was this saying that I will never forget: "Golf reveals your character. Play accordingly." I think about that every time I'm out on the golf course. Robert and I continued our discussion on character and specifically how it affects the building of an effective workforce these days.

Robin: "So while we are on the topic of character, what qualities do you look for when you're building your team? And what skills are hard to find in young professionals today? It seems a lot of people I've been talking to lately just can't seem to figure out the millennial employment personality."

Robert: "Well, there's a true statement if there ever was one! Years ago, I was being interviewed for a job and one of my co-workers I was using as a reference said of me, 'He doesn't have 100% of the experience in everything that you're looking for right this moment. But the kid's got curiosity and massive enthusiasm, and I would take that any day over anything else.' And so, ideally, you would love to say, 'Hey, I'm looking for a square peg,' and if you could find a perfect square peg and it fit in that hole, I'd be very happy. But we really need to be realistic and realize that rarely ever happens. So, you have to begin to think about the compromises you're willing to make. It really depends on the particular role. But, generally, I'm looking for someone who says, 'Okay, I don't have everything, but I'm very enthusiastic about this. I'm committed to working well with others, and I've got serious curiosity. I want to get better at it.' I think those are the key things I look for. The problem with the millennial generation I find is they have a lot of enthusiasm, but it lasts for 15 minutes, and then they want to go learn the next thing."

Robin: "I'm hearing a lot of similar feedback from other recruiters."

Robert: "Years ago, I was at an event in Las Vegas. It was the NRF CIO council. And the panel was talking about the talent gap in IT and recruiting. One gentleman was explaining how he was aligned with the university and trying to recruit candidates out of college. And then this gentleman who worked for Santa Clara University added, 'Yeah, but the kids coming out of college are nowhere near as prepared as they used to be.' He went on to give a thorough description of the fact that many of the new hires today aren't independent decision makers. When you ask a question, they will often text somebody to find the answer. He also pointed out that they were unwilling to stay in a particular position for a reasonable length of time. At that time, we were in a position where we hired a network engineer, and we expected to invest in him, train him, and get him used to our processes and have him in that role for two or three years. The problem is that most of these people coming out of college accept a job and, after six weeks, they expect to move up. There seems to be a total disconnect between reality and expectations."

Robin: "I wonder if that has to do with all the devices everyone is caught up with these days. The average attention span seems to be challenged because devices are always delivering instant gratification."

Robert: "That was one of the many theories of the panel. Another theory was that often when a person competes in sports, they get a medal in 13ᵗʰ place. You're hearing, 'Oh you did good!' There are no objective standards anymore. Everyone is a winner. Also, the good old 'apprentice model' is gone; the model where you learned at the elbow of the expert for years, and then you took it on, you became the master. That thinking doesn't exist anymore. A lot of young people think, 'I can do anything. Then you can pat me on the back, and I get to move on.' And that's the other problem. It seems that the newer workforce generations are requiring a lot of patting on the back for just doing the job you pay them for. Once you've got them as an employee, you have to keep them motivated. I personally have always loved to do nice things for my team that don't fit the classic model of the boss/subordinate relationship. But, on the other hand, I've realized it's become even more important when you're dealing with a lot of youth who still need that pat on the back. We need to say, 'Hey, good job! Thanks for hanging in there! We'll do another one of these in six weeks!'"

Robin: "Yes, thanks for doing what you're paid to do!"

Robert: "Exactly. I've been in senior management meetings and dealing with HR issues for a long time. And lately, we have been noticing how the employee workforce has been developing an entitlement attitude that goes far beyond that basic employment contract that you have as an employee, employer. It has just gotten way out of balance. It doesn't help when you see all the Silicon Valley perks of spas and Jacuzzis in the workplace. Some perks are cool if you can do it. But there comes a point where ultimately you have to focus on the bottom line, and that is that we have to make a profit. Our goal is to serve the customer, who ultimately pays the bills. And there has to be some effort to find a balance in the employment relationship."

Robin: "It's a plus to provide your employees with nice perks, but it's important to keep the overall objective in your sights."

Robert: "Yes. I've never been a boss who tries to micromanage people by closely watching the clock. I'm dealing with creative people and I understand how the creative process works. It doesn't work perfectly on a clock like that. But sometimes there does come a point when employees begin to forget what they're really there to do, which is to contribute to output. And when they're more concerned about the perks and comforts of their work environment than their output, it's gotten excessive. If an organization is too obsessed with employee perks, it's probably not doing the best job it can for its customers."

Robin: "It helps to stay focused on the task at hand when your job is something that fires you up. Having the motivation is a must. So, what is it that fires you up?"

Robert: "I was at a company on the senior management team, and they brought in this chief learning officer to do all these team building exercises. The company was focused on high-performance teams. So, they wanted the senior management team members to know one another. They asked the question, 'What is your personal mantra?' And I thought it was the most frivolous question I had ever heard. The woman asking the questions started on the other side of the room, so I thought I had plenty of time to think of an answer. But, within seconds, she was questioning a person only two people away from me. I thought I better come up with something fast! I suddenly realized she was standing right in front of me. I blurted out, 'I make order out of chaos.' The second I said it aloud, I realized that's exactly what I do. And it puts me in this very interesting intersection between the creative and the process. In my position, I get to help translate what's going on creatively and then try to turn it into a process. Over time, I've come to realize that I get a great deal of satisfaction from making order out of chaos.

"There is the creative side of business where brainstorming takes place and visions come about. It's too early in the process to make sense of it all because it's still being developed. But eventually, the vision becomes a deliverable product that needs to be manufactured. We need to market it, distribute it, sell it, and support it. I sit right at that intersection between the idea and the implementation. I've come to realize that my talents tend to be best applied right there. So, when you ask what motivates me, I'm always sort of subconsciously looking for a chaotic situation that could use some assistance by applying technology to make order out of it."

Robin: "This goes back to your desire and ability to see the big picture and understand how all the pieces of the puzzle fit together to achieve the overall goal. Let's talk middle management. What advice would you give to a talented middle management person who can't seem to break through to the upper management tiers?"

Robert: "I actually had a gentleman work for me at a national retail chain, and he was smart. He looked for a mentor and, for whatever reason, he chose me. And one of the things that I pointed out to him is that curiosity and willingness are the key factors to growth. Because I think there's some of this that you can control. You can create some opportunities for yourself. But there's that famous phrase, too, that the second an opportunity exists and the door swings open, you'd better be ready to jump through it!"

Robin: "Yes! I believe in that. Success is when preparation meets opportunity!"

Robert: "Exactly and I think it's important to maintain curiosity. They should keep showing a willingness to learn as much as they can and to do whatever it takes. Then just be ready for when that moment does arrive. But in some cases, the individual just isn't going to achieve that promotion. It can be for many different reasons: the way the organization is structured, where that person's interests and talents lie, even personality. In certain situations, there's really no growth potential, and it's unlikely that a person will move up the ladder. In those cases, you have to be smart and know when to cut your losses. Sometimes its time to go out and create a new opportunity to set yourself up for better odds of success."

Robin: "It's also compassionate for a boss to be honest and tell the employee when they are on a dead-end path. It could prevent that person from wasting a lot of time in the wrong place."

Robert: "Usually, I spend the time with my employees to try to figure out what is motivating them. So always, what I find first and foremost to be important is whether the organization has what it takes to set them up. I had one guy at an entertainment company who was being very difficult in the very first few days. I finally called him in and I said, 'Hey, let me explain to you where I'm going with the department. Here are the things we're working on. Let me explain to you how you resonate to me. Let me show you the gap between where we're going and where I see you at and help me to understand this gap. Do I have the wrong impression of you? And here's what I think I can do to help you to close the gap. And here's the part that is going to be up to you.' He was actually an extremely talented developer. It's a model that I use all the time."

Robin: "That's really good. I like that a lot."

Robert: "Well, this was many years ago. And this particular talk that I had with this guy turned out very good. We still keep in touch, and he remembers that talk fondly as 'one of Robert's good talks.' I can tell you my success rate with that talk. Almost everyone who I've ever had that talk with has resigned. Another gentleman came in the very next day after this talk, and he said, 'I appreciate everything that you said. I completely understand where you see me. This is not where I want to be. So, I'm giving you my resignation.' Now, the problem with this employee is he was incredibly surly and difficult, and he also held the keys to a lot of technology there. But because of the honest talk, he worked harder in those last two weeks making sure we had a good clean turnover than he worked the rest of the time on the job. The guy just needed to know where he stood. And he needed to be treated respectfully. In the long run, you usually do the person a favor by giving them an out so that they can find where they truly belong."

Unfortunately, treating a person with respect and dignity is sometimes overlooked in the workplace. Being honest and providing an unhappy person with an out can actually be compassionate in the long run. It might be self-serving to keep a person on your team because he's willing to come in and do the job every day. But when a person believes he's made for more and there's no growth potential, honesty is the best policy.

Robin: "What percentage of your time is spent dealing with personalities and making sure you've got the right people in the right positions? You know, casting versus actual execution?"

Robert: "I gave a talk at the Pepperdine School of Management where I spoke about this. I believe my job is 90% psychology, 10% technology. As I've risen through my career, I've understood technology very well. But there is no way any one person in your organization can understand everything about networks, access control lists, security, programming languages, databases, and more. And I've also learned that in an IT organization there are many different personality types. A database administrator is completely different than a network person, than a computer operator, than a programmer, than a business analyst and so forth. So, I've realized I have to understand how they're all working and how I get them motivated toward a common goal. I just realized at one point that my career had become mostly psychologist."

Robin: "What would you say is a major theme of an object lesson you tend to give to your employees?"

Robert: "When I first started as CIO at one of these retail organizations, I met with all the team members and asked the group, 'When someone asks you what you do, how do you respond?' And, of course, a few answered, 'Well I run the network, or I'm a database manager.' I replied, 'Let me give you a different viewpoint. Why don't you say that what you do is you help sell women's clothing and the way you do it is you help with the network or databases.' What I try to do is get them to understand the much bigger picture. You know, the place of employment was not an IT company. It was a women's fashion apparel company, and our job as the IT department was to try to help that come to pass."

Robin: "It seems pretty obvious!"

Robert: "Yes, but sometimes you just need to have a simple conversation, and suddenly the team starts seeing things and behaving differently."

Robin: "Right. It's really about leadership. When they understand the basic rationale, they can get behind the team effort. They've got a reason to do what they do."

Robert: "Yes, and they recognized they weren't just a face in the crowd, but that they actually existed and mattered."

Robin: "How do you want to be remembered?"

Robert: "I would want to be remembered, as fair, inspiring, and a person who always tried to help people achieve the best. And, often times, I look at my position as a coaching job, where I am setting up my employees for as much success as possible by inspiring and encouraging them along the way. When it's all said and done, I didn't write all the software. I didn't keep all the databases and the networks up and running. The staff did that. And it took all of us to cross the finish line together."

Robin: "Very interesting. You know, I agree with so much of your business philosophy. I love your management style. I think when it's all said and done, you're coming from the place of a servant's heart. We serve each other when we are motivated by figuring out how we can help others do better. And when we come from that place, you can't help but succeed. But I'm very excited for you and can't wait to see what the next chapter in your life is going to be!"

JENN HARRIS

Street Swing &
High Heel Golfer

http://streetswings.com
https://highheelgolfer.com

Jenn Harris

*J*en Harris is a young entrepreneur and golf enthusiast who left the corporate world to pursue her dream of sharing her love of golf with others. As an avid golfer, she has spent the past six years bringing the game to non-golfers and showing them how golf can improve their lives by helping them build lasting and rewarding relationships. In 2012, Jenn founded High Heel Golfer, an organization that strives to connect and inspire women to achieve their personal and professional goals through the game of golf. In addition, its program's focus is on personal development, advancement, and mentoring. More recently, Jenn founded Street Swing, a traveling virtual reality golf experience that brings golf directly to the client and their event venues.

BRINGING PROFESSIONAL WOMEN INTO GOLF

I recently had the opportunity to interview Jenn and learn more about her two golf businesses. She explained her mission and vision for both of these exciting golf ventures:

Jenn: "*High Heel Golfer* is helping women learn how to leverage golf for business. It's all about getting women into the game, teaching them the basics, the etiquette, and making them feel comfortable to be able to excel in golf. Women like you and I have been using it to our advantage for years, and a lot of women are simply intimidated by golf. They think, 'No, no, I can't do that,' for a variety of different reasons. So I help them break through those excuses so that they can get out there and experience the same success in building relationships on the course that the rest of us experience. It starts by providing the knowledge that instills confidence. Understanding their fears and giving them the power to overcome these fears helps them to realize that everyone starts somewhere. You begin to realize, if your swing isn't perfect, it's okay. Everybody has a different swing. If you're out there and you feel that everyone's staring at you, it's not because you look silly. It's probably because you're a woman and they're not used to women being out on the golf course. So, it's really just helping them be aware that there is a reason behind everything. And then helping them learn the game as well and feel more comfortable about not being perfect right away, especially if it's not an easy course."

Robin: "What advice would you give to the novice golfer? How can she work her way up to establish relationships with top-tier executives on the golf course?"

Jenn: "So, I would learn the etiquette first. It's okay if you're not a great golfer, but you need to know what is appropriate etiquette on the golf course. You have to start by getting educated on the game. Learn the rules and the jargon. You can pick up a lot from watching the Golf Channel. I wouldn't jump in with the CEOs right away. First, you need to get used to the course and get used to the game. Then, when a CEO or someone does invite you, I would just give full disclosure and ask, 'Is it okay if I'm not a great golfer?' If they say yes, then just go for it. Have fun. Being on the golf course isn't necessarily about your game. It's about how well you connect with others on a personal level."

A VIRTUAL REALITY GOLF EXPERIENCE

Jenn is very fortunate to have successfully merged her love of golf with her career. She will always benefit from the fact that she loves what she does. When you love what you do, you never work a day in your life because you approach every challenge with excitement and positive energy. I asked her about her other business, Street Swings.

Jenn: "*Street Swings* is a golf course experience that comes to you. You could say it's like a golf party bus. We are based out of

San Diego and we have the ability to travel nationwide. I built it because I wanted to create a non-threatening experience to enable people to try golf. We remove the mystery out of everything related to the game. We help the player with everything. They don't need to worry about getting to the golf course, selecting appropriate golf clothing, choosing the right clubs, or learning the game. We bring it all to them. It could be at a corporate headquarters, or we could bring it to a party at the beach, or an event at Petco Park or some other venue. We bring it to where the people are, so they can try out the game and have fun with it. It's pretty much a live-action virtual reality experience, complete with golf instructors on board. So, if a person has never gripped a club or they've never tried to swing, we make it easy. Probably about 50% of the people that have been on the trailer have never picked up a club and they leave saying, 'Wow, this is such a fun game; I never thought I would like this!' I absolutely love introducing people to a game that, for me, has helped build many strong relationships while teaching me strategy and problem-solving skills and building my self-confidence in the process."

Jenn is at a very exciting point in her young entrepreneurial journey. She has accomplished a great deal in just six short years as a golf enthusiast in the industry. In my interview with her, she explained how she is beginning to turn the corner and see the many rewards of carrying out her entrepreneurial mission:

Jenn: "My ultimate goal has always been to help others. It is very rewarding seeing other women have breakthroughs and witness the success they've achieved. My investment in my clients has enabled them to develop and build relationships with their bosses, clients and others. With *Street Swings*, my recent mission of helping underprivileged kids is super rewarding! Showing those kids how to play golf can change their paths and their lives. They come from hard circumstances. They've been dealt challenging hands. If I can give them a path out of poverty and get them into a life-changing program, that's all the reward I need! It's very exciting that we have a virtual reality game that they enjoy and want to play. That's where it begins. The self-confidence that is instilled in them through my program leads to their desire to learn more, be disciplined, study more, and be more. This can change their whole trajectory. Because of the value of these lessons, they may be inspired to go to college, and set and achieve goals. This is the most rewarding thing for me, to be a part of this transformational success!"

Robin: "What got you started in golf and how has it contributed to your success in business?"

Jenn: "My dad got me into golf at a young age, and I think it was how I spent quality time with him, which was nice. As a kid in a busy family, it's hard to spend hours and hours together, so playing golf gave me that access to my dad, which was really great. The way it contributed to my success was really twofold. One, it helped me feel comfortable around anyone. Sometimes in business, we meet people with impressive titles, such as VP or CEO. Those who have powerful titles and the experience to match intimidate many younger people. But on the golf course, it levels the playing field and we're all the same. Sometimes, I might even be a little bit better. So golf put me at ease and allowed me to be myself around people from all walks of life. The second thing is that it helped me overcome challenges and learn how to take smart risks. With golf, strategy is an important element of the game. A good player has to maneuver through the course, solving problems along the way. So strategy is key."

Robin: "Often, entrepreneurs back into their circumstances in a creative way. As an avid golfer and entrepreneur myself, I'm curious about what led you to start your business. Also, what motivates you to go to work every day as a sort of 'golf evangelist,' helping to raise awareness of this rewarding sport?"

Jenn: "Those are great questions! It definitely wasn't intentional, but I didn't come to this by accident either. I'm the type of person that likes to dive right in. So, when I have an idea, I just jump right in, and I figure it out as I go. As for motivation, there are two reasons why I do what I do. The first thing that motivates me is my desire to help people grow and be successful. And so, with the game of golf, if I can help people connect with others and, as a result, grow their businesses, I have accomplished what I set out to do. This goes for children too! Golf opens doors for them as well. We're planning to do some work with Pro-Kids which is The First Tee of San Diego this year. Their mission is to challenge underserved youth to excel in life by promoting character development, life skills, and values through education and the game of golf. If what I'm doing can help these kids out of poverty and into the game of golf, amazing things will follow. This is a major motivating factor for me in pursuing this dream every day. The second motivator is that I love creating things. I wanted to be an inventor as a little kid. I like taking an idea and making it a reality. Being able to design and develop a trailer that pops up and lets you play golf anywhere, anytime, has been so much fun for me. Being able to engineer the design to solve a variety of problems using many different innovative methods is very satisfying. I love building, creating, and problem solving. So, I'm fortunate that I love what I do."

A WINNING ATTITUDE

In an earlier chapter, my friend Hyrum W. Smith, the highly successful entrepreneur and global leader in corporate training, emphasized the importance of attitude. He warned against what he called negative "self-talk." We agreed that perception often becomes reality. If you think you can't succeed, there is a very good chance you will fail! A negative self-perception could be very destructive toward achieving a goal. As a young entrepreneur, Jenn has person-

ally learned that lesson. I asked her about the obstacles that she has had to overcome to find her path to success. She explained:

Jenn: "In the past, I sometimes lacked confidence in what value I could bring to a project or a situation. It's a terribly negative way to feel and can be damaging to the success of a mission. To make matters worse, I had a bad habit of taking things personally when someone didn't want my product right then and there, on the spot. I've gotten rid of that way of thinking. Learning to overcome those insecurities has had a huge impact on my ability to succeed. These were thought habits that I had to replace. And by breaking that cycle, I am able to be a positive force for others, helping them to meet their own challenges and making a big impact on their lives."

Robin: "So you agree that a positive attitude is critical for success in business?"

Jenn: "Absolutely! I've replaced the negative with the positive. Now I refuse to give up and I'm no longer inhibiting myself from success by self-imposed limitations. My biggest factor in achieving success is my inability to hear the word 'no.' In most cases, that word just doesn't exist for me! People will say, 'We can't do that,' and I'll say, 'Yes, we can!' For example, we just did a major 45-day tour in New York. I had these guys packing the trailer for the trip and they were saying, 'There's no way we're going to get all this stuff inside the trailer!' I refused to entertain the idea that it was impossible. Of course, with some persistence, there absolutely was a way to get everything in the trailer. In fact, by the time the trailer was completely packed and ready for the trip, about a third of the trailer was still empty. So, I've learned not to listen to people when they are negative.

"When I built the trailer, I was so focused on what the trailer was designed to do; I didn't focus on the fact that it had to be driven. So, when it was time to get it out on the road, not knowing how to drive a trailer was an issue but not a deterrent. There was a time for me when not knowing how to drive a huge trailer may have been a very discouraging thing. But with my positive way of looking at things, the solution was simple. I had to learn how to drive it. It was scary at first. But like everything, including golf, it's by doing it that you overcome the fear and get the task done."

Robin: "Successful entrepreneurs usually can point to a mentor or another figure in their lives who gave them that initial break and made their business possible. Is there a particular person to whom you attribute your start? Someone who inspired you to take the risk and embrace the challenge?"

Jenn: "I attribute my initial success to the support of my family, and in particular, my dad. When I came up with the idea, he was all for it. He's helped me get it off the ground by investing in my business. He said, 'Okay, you want to do this, go do it!' That really tells me that he believes in my abilities. So that's been huge. If I had to get a traditional business loan, it would have required many more hoops, and it would've taken a lot longer. I couldn't have jumped in and launched as quickly as I did."

VALUE IN COACHES & MENTORS

Robin: "What about ongoing support and guidance? Do you have a business coach?"

Jenn: "There are definitely those coaches who have taught me how to have the winning attitude that's so crucial for success. They're the ones who have helped me work on my self-perception. There are also the practical advisors who have taught me many useful things like how to drive the trailer, how to operate a generator, and what to do when a fuse blows. I've had to learn about electrical engineering and kilowatts and amperage. I needed to learn it all for myself so that I could understand and be able to create the right programs for my customers. So all of my advisors bring different knowledge and experience to my businesses. And collectively, there is a lot of intelligence among us. It's nice to know I'm not alone, and if I get stuck with something, one of these people will have the answer. It helps me to have the confidence to know that with perseverance and proper guidance, I can do just about anything."

GROW WITH WHAT YOU KNOW

Robin: "How do you generate new and innovative ideas to diversify your business further and expand your offerings?"

Jenn: "As for innovation, it's interesting that many new ideas usually originate from conversations I have had with my customers and potential clients. So, when I'm planning an event with them or discussing what we do, it's really in understanding what they need and how we can provide that for them that spawns the ideas. Sometimes, their vision becomes part of my next product strategy. With *High Heel Golfer*, a woman said, 'I would love it if I had a card that told me all the club distances.' And that became the very next product we offered, and women love it! Inspiration for new ideas and product offerings often comes from customer feedback. I may be chatting with a customer and answering a question when suddenly an idea will come to me on how to make the user experience even better. I may be inspired to shoot a video or add something to the trailer. Whatever the idea may be, I usually act on that inspiration.

"Innovation also occurs when I'm trying to solve problems. Sometimes, in just communicating a need to another person, an idea will suddenly come to me. But usually I'll share a challenge with a mentor or advisor, and the brainstorming begins, and together we find solutions. Often, those solutions involve new customer choices."

GOLF AS A PEOPLE CONNECTOR

Robin: "How instrumental was networking through golf to your initial success?"

Jenn: "So, networking is huge. Something that I didn't realize in the beginning but realize now is that networking is less about selling. When I first started networking, I wanted everyone to learn about *High Heel Golfer*. But over time, I realized the more significant goal of networking is connecting on a personal level and getting to know someone. It's gratifying to connect with a person and learn that we have similarities that are outside of business. Networking through golf has helped me to find good friends who I just enjoy hanging out with. When people I play golf with actually become friends, and I start to understand their businesses better, I try to look at how can I connect them with others; how can I help them succeed? And they're going to do the same for me. So, networking is not really about selling. It's not such a hard sell when I'm networking to build relationships. That's really easy on the golf course because you have four or five hours. You're not going to talk about golf or business the whole time. You really get to know about people, and you get to have fun with them, joke about their swing, and communicate about so many different things. So, the golf course is probably the easiest place to truly connect with others. But now that I work in the golf industry, networking plays a smaller part. I serve the golfer. It's ironic. It helped me a lot personally when I was in corporate America."

Robin: "Explain to me how golf helped you network when you were in corporate America."

Jenn: "When I was in corporate America, networking through golf was so much more relevant to my position. But, as far as networking goes, I'd say, be careful not to over-network. A lot of people will go to several networking events a week, and then they don't have the time or the energy actually to follow up and connect. Just going and playing golf with someone once isn't enough. You have to follow up with that person. Maybe go grab a coffee and find out more specifically how you can really help. Try to connect on a deeper, more serious level. A person is better off picking just a few events and investing in quality relationships rather than quantity. You can come back from an event with a big stack of business cards. But then what are you going to do with them? Are you going to spam them? That's hardly the way to develop lasting relationships. But since I left corporate and began serving the golf industry, it's less about my own networking and more about connecting other golfers with each other so that they can build mutually beneficial relationships."

Robin: "Can you tell me more about that?"

Jenn: "Actually, this year I'm starting an ambassador program to provide an opportunity for all of my contacts who believe in this program – believe in *Street Swings*, to come together and find others to develop relationships that are mutually beneficial to their businesses. So, if they help spread the word about *Street Swings*, I'm offering this networking venue of highly engaged business professionals where they might find some lasting partnerships. I want them to become part of my tribe and, by having these mutual interests, they can connect with others who are like-minded people. They can make true connections by attending my events."

IF I KNEW THEN WHAT I KNOW NOW

Robin: "That sounds awesome! Since you were in the corporate world and left, this may be a great question to get your perspective. What advice would you give to a middle management person who has basically hit the wall and wants to either move up in his career or do something else like strike out on his own?"

Jenn: "I would do a lot of research. I would not be like me and just jump in. Unless you have unlimited resources and are in a position to take on the risk, I would research so you know what you're getting yourself into. Another thing I would recommend is learning how to sell. I think one of the most important things to know when starting your own business is how to sell. I have had to learn that the hard way and so I think I would've been more successful, more quickly if I had approached this venture with sharp selling skills from the beginning. But I'm okay with the speed of my success. I know everything will come at the right time. But since cash flow is very important to the success of any business, understanding how to sell is very important. In order to do that successfully, you need to be able to define your product and your market. And since every product is evolving, you need to have the vision to know how the needs of your market will change over time. These are important factors in sales.

"Also, as a new entrepreneur in my journey as a business owner, there was a certain level of dissatisfaction I had with myself. There seemed to be something that was holding me back from being the best that I knew I could be. In my case, I wanted to improve my sales skills. So, I went on a retreat to better understand this. I took the time to analyze my progress and shortfalls to figure out how I could ultimately do better. By journaling, I became acutely aware of the things in my life that were holding me back. This experience has taught me that we all have stuff that tends to hold us back by competing for our energy. By identifying those distractions that interfere with our success, we can free our time to sharpen our skills and become even better. It's very liberating to dump the baggage that holds us back and focus our energy on the things that help us to achieve our goals."

Robin: "What qualities do you look for when you are trying to build a team? What skills are hard to find in young professionals today?"

Jenn: "I'm not going to lie. This is a very difficult thing for me. I have not figured it out yet. I've brought a couple of people on, and I think a lot of people are really good at selling themselves, and I think they're going to be able to do the job, and then I find out they can't. So, I really haven't totally figured that part out yet. One quality that is hard to find in a person is someone who can truly be a self-starter, especially coming from the perspective of the entrepreneur. It's not easy to find someone who's willing to be creative and solve problems autonomously. But I'm realizing that a lot of people need guidance, especially if they're working under me because they don't have that entrepreneurial spirit that just likes to figure things out."

Robin: "Jenn, after 25 years, I haven't figured it out either! Maybe it's a matter of learning to be a better leader on our end. Well, this is my last question. How do you want to be remembered?"

Jenn: "I want to be remembered as someone who's a great connector. Someone who people can trust to help them connect and develop winning relationships with the right people for a mutually beneficial and lasting relationship. I also want to be remembered as someone who helps others succeed – helps them achieve their goals. Those are the two things I want people to remember me by."

Robin: "That's awesome. We seem to have a lot in common because I share those sentiments! I'm so excited for you and for your two ventures. I just love seeing how *High Heel Golfer* has led to the development of *Street Swings*! You're on such a great journey, and I think this year is going to be an amazing year for you! So, I just can't wait to see what's going to happen next."

PRACTICAL TIPS TO GET YOU STARTED

For the Women: Forward Tees Advantage

(<u>Attention Men</u>: Learn how having a woman golfer play in your foursome can help you win big!)

Robin playing golf in Cabo

very golf course has different sets of tees for golfers of varying skill levels to play. The skill level for each set of tees is designated by the color of the tee markers. Typically, there are three sets of tees: the forward tees, (closest to the green), the middle tees (second closest to the green) and the back tees, (furthest from the green.) It is customary for women to use the forward tees, (also known as the red tees or the women's tees). This can result in as much as a 100-yard advantage on the initial drive. This is a tremendous benefit because it can make a big difference in your drive and provides women the opportunity to be more competitive among men.

Charity golf events usually involve the more casual format of a scramble. In a scramble, players play in teams, usually foursomes. All four team members tee off, and they choose the location of the best ball from where all players take their next shot. This format is called "best ball." In a scramble, since women tee off from the forward tees, a decent woman golfer is in a good position to have the best ball, advancing the team to the most favorable position. Men love playing with good female golfers because that immediate 100-yard advantage into a par five puts us in a good position to make an eagle. As a woman, if you play well from the forward tees, you will be asked time and again to play in charity events because men love that advantage! You will have the opportunity to make great connections and build lasting relationships!

NETWORKING OPTIONS FOR NON-GOLFERS
Sponsorships

Wearable Imaging Hole Sponsor

The power of golf has such influence that it reaches beyond golfers to non-golfing participants! Even if you don't play, you can participate through your business or employer's business by getting involved in charity tournaments. One of the best ways to do this is through a sponsorship option. You don't have to know anything about golf. Find charities that are holding golf tournaments in your area. Call them up and inquire about the various options for sponsorship. You can usually sponsor a hole, or become a higher-level sponsor. There is something for every advertising budget. For my particular business, this type of advertising is typically more effective than other options such as print ads, broadcast media, or direct mail. But do your own homework. There are options that are inexpensive enough for you to conduct your own test and compare the results to your normal advertising vehicles.

SPONSORING A HOLE

Wearable Imaging booth at a charity event

122

One of the more cost-effective sponsorship options in which my company enjoys success is sponsoring a hole. Wearable Imaging will typically sponsor a hole in a charity golf tournament with a scramble format. In a scramble, there are 144 players, and there are eight people who tee off on each of 18 holes. So, there is a continuous stream of foursomes that come past your booth. A short distance from the tee, we set up a table with brochures and promotional items to distribute to the players. We staff the booth with our knowledgeable team who can concisely convey the benefits of our promotional products and answer any questions. We collect business cards for prize drawings, and we even have a wheel that participants can spin for a chance to win more valuable promotional gifts. Each foursome must come past our booth as they play through. We have an opportunity to talk to 144 tournament participants who are usually influential members of the local business community. In addition, we capture their contact information, and they leave with ours. It's a great way to connect with influencers and high-level corporate decision makers!

HIGHER LEVEL SPONSORSHIPS

If your company has a larger budget and is looking to increase brand awareness, there are usually various levels of sponsorship opportunities available. The top sponsor is called the title sponsor, which gets brand exposure just about everywhere. The title sponsorship involves much larger dollar amounts and a higher level of brand exposure. Depending on the tournament, media exposure could include broadcast and print media, press releases, websites, and a variety of local media advertising. These higher dollar donors also benefit from large banner displays and branded promotional giveaways at the event. Sponsorship ranges are very broad, so find out what options are available based on the charity that interests you.

Robin's foursome at Pelican Hill Golf Club

NO COST OPTIONS!

Looking for a way to get involved that is completely cost-free to you, your business, or your employer's company? Participate as a volunteer! There are several volunteer opportunities at a charity golf tournament. These charity event coordinators need people to help with member check-in, manage the raffles, organize the silent auctions, even be a hole-in-one witness. I would recommend a person contact the event coordinator to find out what types of volunteer opportunities exist. Don't be fooled and dismiss this option as a "non-player" activity. Most charity events host high-level business executives because corporations typically buy foursomes and the execs are the ones who go and play. I have met hundreds of amazing people at these tournaments. Players are generally in a generous mood when they hit the links for charity. This could be the opportunity for the break you've been looking for!

NETWORKING TIPS FOR GOLFERS
ESTABLISH A HANDICAP

There are several myths out there about establishing handicaps. The most common two myths are: 1) it's expensive because it involves club membership, and 2) you have to be a good golfer. First, let's dispel the club membership myth. The term "club" does not refer to an actual place, such as a country club, but to a licensed club of members authorized by the USGA. These clubs are usually associated with golf courses but can also be virtual. There are many online apps associated with these clubs to help you keep track of your scores. Every time you play, you enter your scorecard information. The app generates your handicap index by applying a formula to the relevant score information of your ten best scores of the previous 20 rounds. It also takes into consideration soft measures such as the difficulty of the course. The expense is a modest annual fee ranging somewhere around $30 to $60. With smartphone apps, keeping track of your handicap index is a very easy thing to do.

There are several reasons to establish a golf handicap. First of all, it helps you to become a better golfer by keeping you aware of your progress and motivating you to compete against yourself. In addition, it is required if you want to play in any official tournament. One of the best reasons is that when you are comparing your performance to that of your friends and associates, the handicap index makes it an 'apples to apples' comparison by taking into consideration other factors to level the playing field. To learn more, visit https://www.usga.org.

PLAY AS A SINGLE & HIT THE DRIVING RANGE

Charity tournaments are a great way to meet people and give back to charity. At a charity golf tournament, players can sign up as a single where they are joined with other golfers usually in a foursome. I've used this networking technique often. Typically, I would be paired with three other guys. They were probably thinking, "Who is this girl teeing off from the red tees?" Then I would get up there and smack the ball 250 yards. Suddenly, there was a newfound respect and intrigue. So, being able to hit the ball a good distance was often a great conversation starter that led to all kinds of interesting discussions. However, anyone placed on a team with three others suddenly has a common interest with those members and conversation becomes very natural.

If you want to go out and play 18 holes, late Friday afternoon is a great time to hit the local public golf course and play as a single. They usually have great deals at that time, and it's often a good time to meet professionals taking off early from work for the weekend. I've met some really great people playing as a single. Also, if you're a (single) single, this is a great way to meet new people – and who knows, it may even lead to a date! The driving range is a great option for evening practice. Every golf course has night range hours and with that often comes social opportunities. Everyone is there for the same reason. They want to improve their swing. I've met some really nice people at the driving range. Sometimes, groups end up meeting up at the bar for drinks afterward.

EVERYONE WAS ONCE A BEGINNER

Often, when I ask a person why they don't play golf, I hear the excuse, "Because I'm not good enough." I don't believe that's a valid reason because golf is a journey, not a destination. If you understand the game and the etiquette, the skill will come with time. My most favorite golf course experiences usually have nothing to do with the skill level of the people with whom I'm playing. In my experience, some of the best times I've spent have been with golfers who are at the beginning skill levels.

As we discuss throughout this book, although golf is a rewarding game, it's the significance of the relationships built through golf that have the true lasting value. Golf is an excellent vehicle for recreation, socializing, and especially building relationships. So don't rob yourself of the opportunity to develop valuable relationships by avoiding a game you think you are not good enough to play. Yes, you need a basic level of understanding and etiquette before you get on the course. At the end of this chapter, I have provided many resources for you to obtain those beginner level skills. So, please don't let your lack of skill or knowledge be a deterrent to improving your life through golf.

If you are starting out and want to learn to play, I highly recommend you contact your local public golf course to find out about lessons. There are usually two types of lessons: private lessons and group lessons. Group lessons are less expensive and can be a lot of fun. Sign up with a friend if you're a little shy or intimidated. The buddy system is often a good way to experience something new.

Once you get to know and understand the basics, get out there and enjoy your time on the course. You will not believe that you waited this long to embark on this rewarding journey. So, put aside the excuses and get moving. Like everything else in life, it involves one step at a time.

THERE ARE REALLY
19 HOLES IN GOLF!

After spending five hours on the course, it's finally time for a cocktail! The 19th hole is the place to unwind after a fun day on the course. This is another name for the restaurant or bar located at the course. It's a great opportunity to enjoy your foursome, to bond, talk about your round, and get to know one another on a deeper level.

When you play in charity events, they usually have a dinner and a silent auction, followed by awards and announcing the auction winners and a speaker talking about the charity.

Some of my greatest friendships and business connections were first formed on the golf course, but I also have great memories of the 19th hole! Like the time I had my first hole in one and had to buy drinks for everyone! That is customary when you have a hole in one; you owe the entire bar a round of drinks!!!

The 19th hole provides a special opportunity to get to know your new friends better and continue to build relationships. Many of these will continue to flourish through the years. You'll be glad you made it to the 19th hole!

I would love to hear from you; now it's time to write your story. Whether you decide to try out the sport for the very first time or this inspires you to get out and play more or get involved in charity golf events, I want to hear your story! I want to be writing about you in my next book J

Email me: Robin@thegolfcoursemillionaire.com

Robin with friends at the 19th hole

RESOURCE GUIDE

Where to Find Lessons:

https://www.pga.com/play-golf-america

Jane Rosenberg is my teaching pro. She is amazing! She is located in the Orange County, CA area www.janerosenberggolf.com email: jane@janerosenberggolf.com

Golf Networking for Men

https://www.meetup.com/topics/social-golf-networking/

Resources for Women:

Executive Women's Golf Association /EWGA

Whether you are just learning to play, improving and learning new skills, or are already an accomplished golfer, EWGA is THE Golf Community for you!

http://www.ewga.com

Women On Course/ WOC

Women on Course is a dynamic national community of diverse and influential women built around interactive lifestyle and work-style events with opportunities to create connections, deepen relationships and develop personal and professional skills.

https://www.womenoncourse.com

High Heel Golfer

High Heel Golfer strives to connect and inspire women to achieve their personal and professional goals. In addition, its programs focus on personal development, advancement, and mentoring.

https://highheelgolfer.com

Virtual Golf Bus – Book for Events

http://streetswings.com

Establish a Handicap

http://www.usga.org

https://www.usga.org/articles/2015/03/want-to-establish-a-handicap-index--join-the-club.html

http://www.usga.org/HDCPLicensedAssoc/licensed_associations.asp

Search for Local Golf Tournaments:

Find a new golfing buddy, compete in events across the country.

https://golftourney.com

Book Tee Times at a Discount:

https://www.teeoff.com

15 Ways To Play Golf at a Discount:

https://www.golfdigest.com/gallery/15-ways-to-play-golf-on-the-cheap

Best Places to Buy Golf Clothes & Equipment:

https://www.worldwidegolfshops.com/

http://www.pgatoursuperstore.com/index.jsp

Top Golf Magazines:

https://www.golfdigest.com/magazine

http://www.golf.com

https://womensgolfjournal.com

Purchase Unique Tournament Tee Prize / Items for Golf:

http://www.wearableimaging.com

Purchase Promotional Items to Get Your Business Noticed:

http://www.wearableimaging.com

Connect with Robin Richter on www.LinkedIn.com:

https://www.linkedIn.com/in/robinkrallrichter/

Robin@thegolfcoursemillionaire.com

Affiliate Charities

Golf Fore Africa (Charity of golf pro & hall of famer, Betsy King)

http://www.golfforeafrica.org

Alzheimer's Orange County

https://www.alzoc.org (Robin Richter & Wearable Imaging, Inc. are proud supporters.)

Book signing

Robin & Jamee winning the SDG&E tournament

Robin & MLB Hall of Famer Rod Carew's daughter

Matt and Robin

Robin and her dad in the early 90s

Robin and Matt Richter

Robin playing golf in Palos Verdes

Robin playing with her foursome at a charity golf tournament

Mike Rees feeding Robin's husky head cover

CONNECT WITH ROBIN

E-mail Robin@thegolfcoursemillionaire.com

Linked In https://www.linkedIn.com/in/robinkrallrichter/

Website www.wearableimaging.com

141

Made in the USA
Columbia, SC
21 April 2019